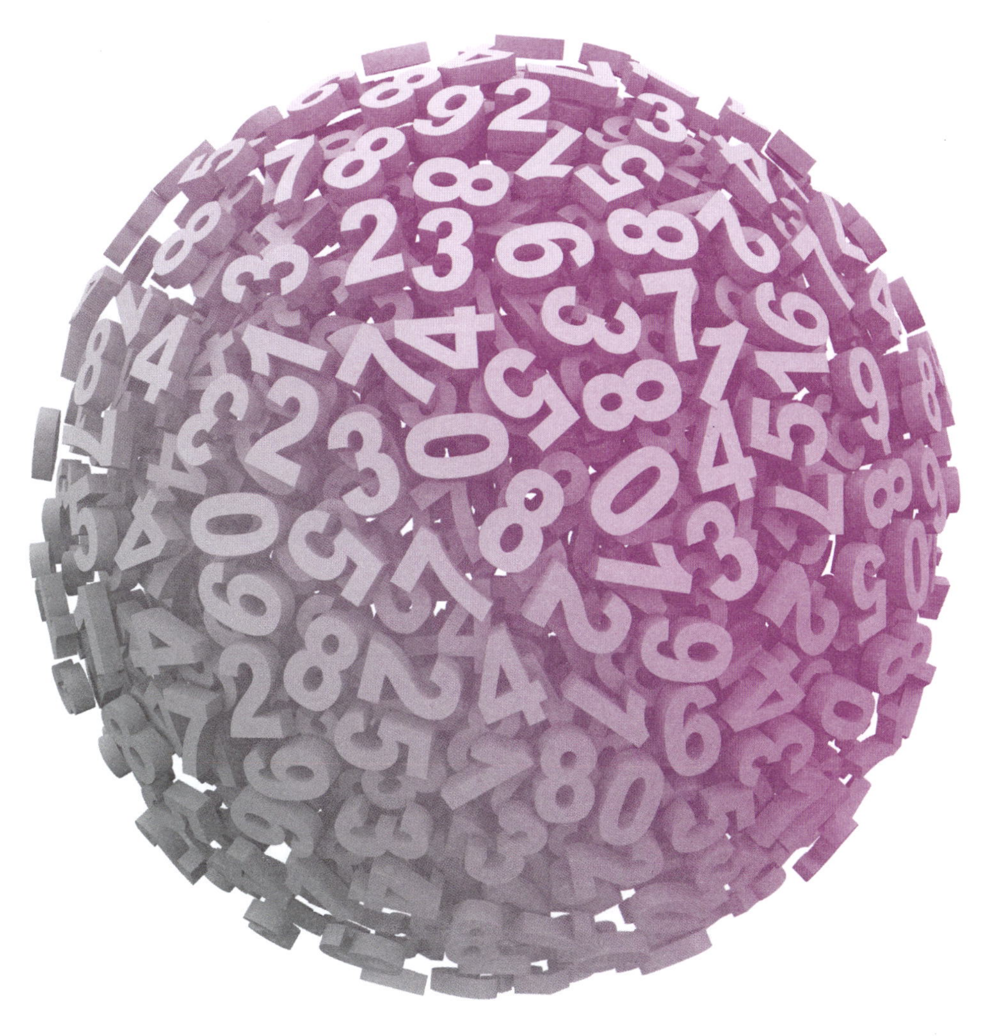

NUMBER 5+

Walker Maths Essentials: Number 5+
1st Edition
Charlotte Walker
Victoria Walker

Designer: Cheryl Smith, Macarn Design
Production controller: Michelle Gordon

Any URLs contained in this publication were checked for currency during the production process. Note, however, that the publisher cannot vouch for the ongoing currency of URLs.

Acknowledgements
Cover photo courtesy of Shutterstock.
We wish to thank the Boards of Trustees of Darfield and Riccarton High Schools for allowing us to use materials and ideas developed while teaching. Our thanks also go to all past and present colleagues, especially Kath Wilson, who have generously shared their experience and ideas.

For product information and technology assistance,
in Australia call **1300 790 853**;
in New Zealand call **0800 449 725**

For permission to use material from this text or product, please email **aust.permissions@cengage.com**

National Library of New Zealand Cataloguing-in-Publication Data
A catalogue record for this book is available from the National Library of New Zealand.
978 0 17044701 0

Cengage Learning Australia
Level 7, 80 Dorcas Street
South Melbourne, Victoria Australia 3205

Cengage Learning New Zealand
Unit 4B Rosedale Office Park
331 Rosedale Road, Albany, North Shore 0632, NZ

For learning solutions, visit **cengage.co.nz**

Printed in China by 1010 Printing International Limited.
2 3 4 5 6 7 24

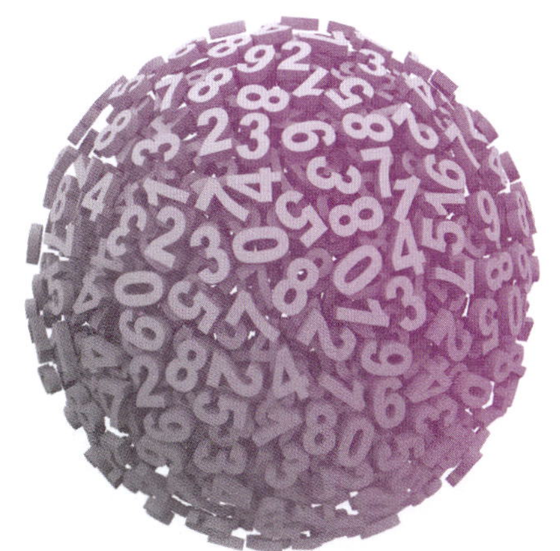

CONTENTS

ISBN: 9780170447010

Glossary

Make your own glossary of key terms:

Term	Definition	Picture/Example
BEDMAS		
Integers		
Multiple		
Lowest common multiple (LCM)		
Factor		
Highest common factor (HCF)		
Prime number		
Square root		
Consecutive		
Adjacent		
Numerator		
Denominator		

ISBN: 9780170447010

Mixed fraction		
Improper fraction		
Reciprocal		
Equivalent fraction		
Place value		
Decimal place		
Significant figure		
Recurring decimal		
Ratio		
$>$		
$<$		
$\geq$		
$\leq$		

ISBN: 9780170447010

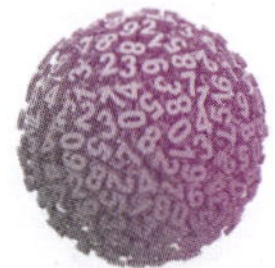

The language of mathematics

Words to operations

Write down the most appropriate operation (**+**, **–**, **x** or **÷**) for each of the following terms.

	Terms	Operations
1	If 0.45 is **decreased by** two tenths, what is the result?	–
2	Calculate one eighth **and** a half.	
3	Find 0.3 **multiplied by** 0.4.	
4	Calculate the **difference between** a half and a third.	
5	Twelve is **added** to negative five.	
6	What is 0.12 **increased by** a quarter?	
7	Find a tenth **divided by** four.	
8	What is 0.15 **plus** a half?	
9	Find a number that is **smaller than** 0.01.	
10	Find the result when an eighth is **reduced by** a tenth.	
11	What is 0.71 **more than** a quarter?	
12	What is the **total of** a third and 0.2?	
13	Find a half **of** a sixth.	
14	Calculate a half **less than** five eighths.	
15	What is nine **times** a quarter?	
16	Find the **sum of** 0.002 and 0.35.	
17	What is twenty-seven eighths **shared between** four?	
18	0.92 **subtracted** from 0.5.	
19	What is the **product** of 1.6 and eleven?	

  ISBN: 9780170447010

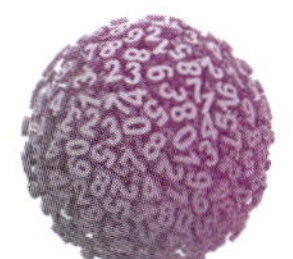

Integers

Adding and subtracting

- **–** means move **left**.
- **+** means move **right**.
- Remember that **– – = +.**

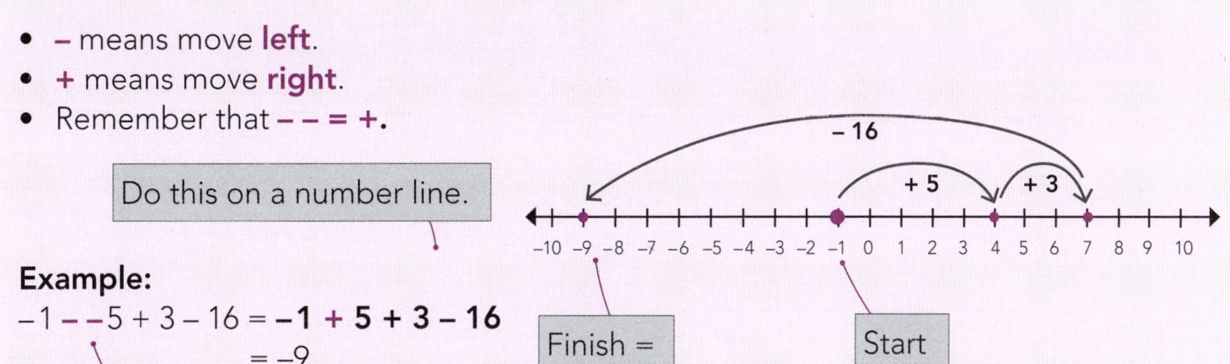

Example:

–1 **– –**5 + 3 – 16 = **–1 + 5 + 3 – 16**

= –9

– – ⇒ +

Write the calculation and answer shown by each diagram (start at the big dot).

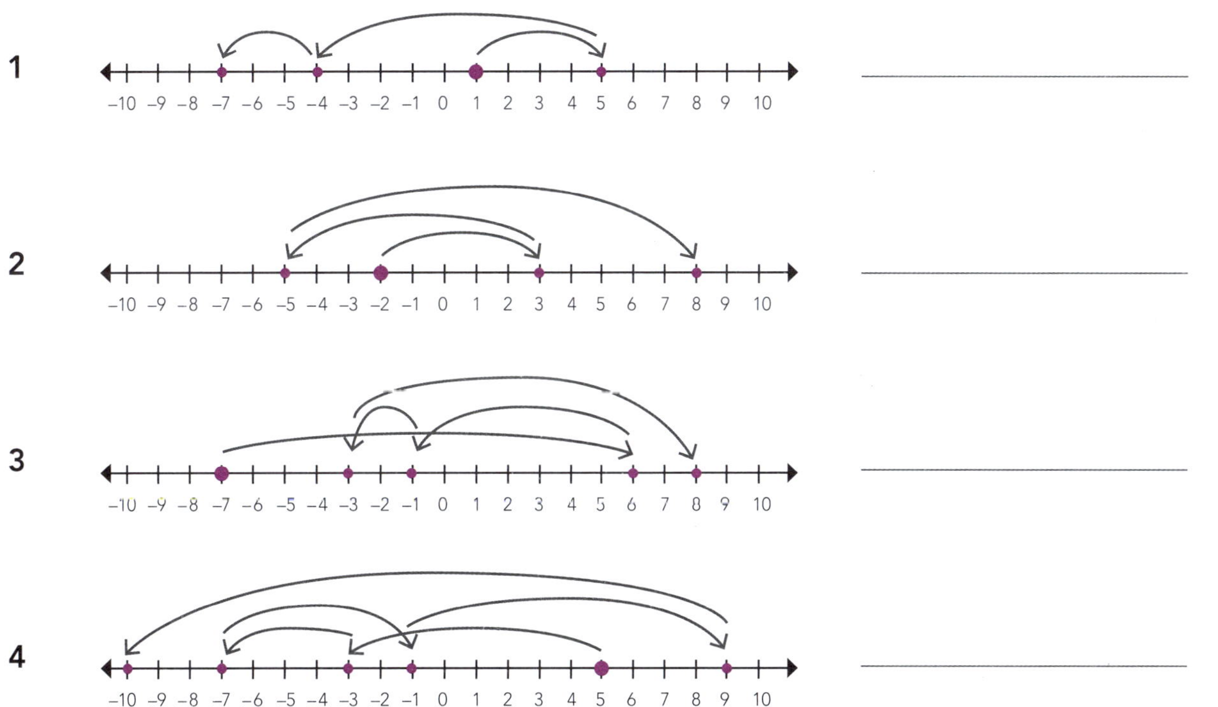

1 ______________________

2 ______________________

3 ______________________

4 ______________________

You should be able to find more than one answer to **5** and **6**. Check your answers with your neighbour.

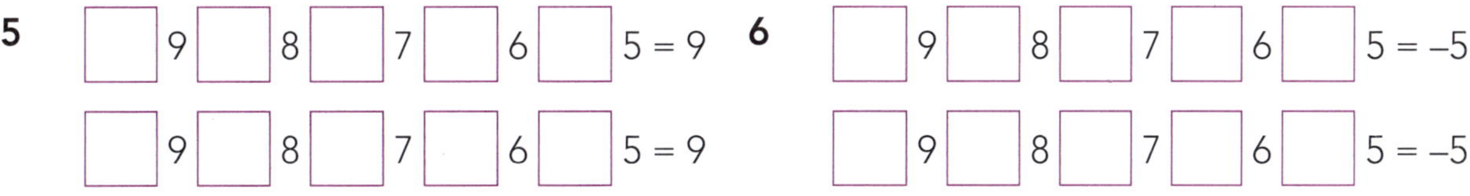

5 ☐ 9 ☐ 8 ☐ 7 ☐ 6 ☐ 5 = 9

☐ 9 ☐ 8 ☐ 7 ☐ 6 ☐ 5 = 9

6 ☐ 9 ☐ 8 ☐ 7 ☐ 6 ☐ 5 = –5

☐ 9 ☐ 8 ☐ 7 ☐ 6 ☐ 5 = –5

ISBN: 9780170447010

Multiplying and dividing

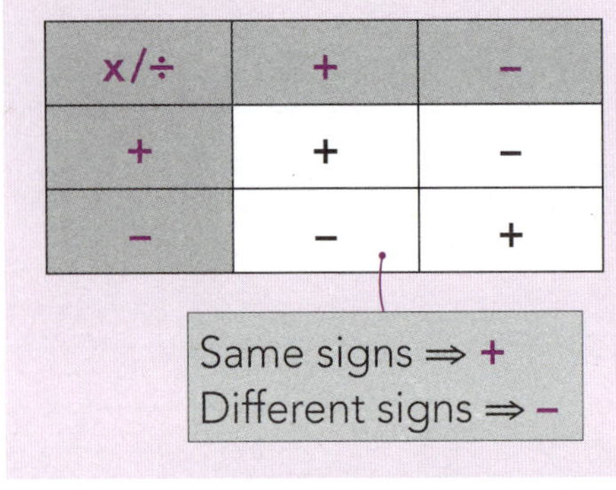

x/÷	+	–
+	+	–
–	–	+

Example: $-1 \times -6 \div 3 \times -7 = (-1 \times -6) \div 3 \times -7$

$= (6 \div 3) \times -7$

$= 2 \times -7$

$= -14$

If there is more than one multiply or divide sign, work from left to right.

Highlight the correct answer for each of the following.

1	$-18 \div 2 \times -3$	3	–27
		27	–3
3	$4 \times -3 \div -12 \times -2$	$\frac{1}{2}$	$-\frac{1}{2}$
		2	–2

2	$-2 \times 24 \div -4 \times 3$	–4	–36
		36	4
4	$-24 \div 6 \times -2 \div -1$	–8	8
		–1	1

Calculate the following.

5 $-8 \times 4 \div -2 \times -1 =$ ____________

6 $-12 \div -3 \times 6 \div 2 =$ ____________

7 $20 \div -4 \times -6 \times -2 =$ ____________

8 $-96 \div -24 \div 4 \div -2 =$ ____________

Mixing it up

1 The temperature in the evening was 3°C. During the night, the temperature dropped by 11°C. What was the temperature in the morning?

____

2 A lift starts at the ground floor (floor 0), goes up seven floors, down four floors, up one floor, and down another two floors. What floor does it finish on?

____

3 Mark owes his mum $65. He does three hours' housework for which he is paid $12 per hour, and then borrows another $20 from her. How much does he still owe his mum?

____

4 A scuba diver is at a depth of 22 m. She descends 6 m, then another 3 m, and then ascends to 5 m below the surface. How far below the surface is she?

____

ISBN: 9780170447010

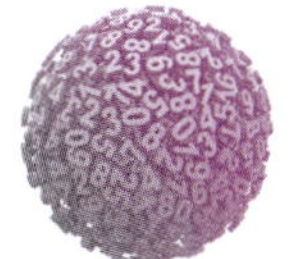

Types of numbers

Multiples

- Multiples of a number are the results of multiplying the number by another number.

Examples: The multiples of **3** are: **3**, **6**, **9**, **12**, **15**, ...
The multiples of **5** are: **5**, **10**, **15**, **20**, ...

These are the answers from the times tables.

1 Complete the table.

Number	First five multiples
2	2, 4, 6, 8, 10
11	
13	
25	

2 Complete the table by stating if these are true or false.

Statement	True or False
111 is a multiple of 3	
91 is a multiple of 7	
92 is a multiple of 8	
10 is a multiple of 1	

Lowest common multiple (LCM)
The lowest common multiple of two numbers is the **smallest multiple** of **both** numbers.

Example: The multiples of **7** are 7, 14, 21, 28, 35, 42, 49, **56**, 63, ..., **112**, ...
The multiples of **8** are 8, 16, 24, 32, 40, 48, **56**, 64, ..., **112**, ...
The multiples they have in **common** (are on both lists) are **56**, **112**, ...
The **lowest common multiple** of **7** and **8** is **56**.

Write enough multiples of these numbers in order to highlight common ones, and identify the lowest.

3 Multiples of 6: ______________________
Multiples of 5: ______________________
The lowest common multiple of 6 and 5 is: __________

4 Multiples of 9: ______________________
Multiples of 7: ______________________
The lowest common multiple of 9 and 7 is: __________

5 Multiples of 12: ______________________
Multiples of 8: ______________________
The lowest common multiple of 12 and 8 is: __________

6 Multiples of 4: ______________________
Multiples of 13: ______________________
The lowest common multiple of 4 and 13 is: __________

ISBN: 9780170447010

Factors

- Factors of a number are all the numbers that **divide** into it exactly.

Example: The factors of **8** are: **1**, **2**, **4**, 8.
The factors of **12** are: **1**, **2**, 3, **4**, 6, 12.

- The **common factors** of two numbers are those that are **factors of both**.

Example: The common factors of **8** and **12** are **1**, **2** and **4** because they are on both lists.

1 Complete the table.

Number	Factors
20	1, 2, 4, 5, 10, 20
18	
23	
60	

2 Are the following statements true or false?

Statement	True or False
3 is a factor of 27	
1 is a factor of 17	
6 is a factor of 130	
15 is a factor of 175	

Highest common factor (HCF)

- The highest common factor of two numbers is the **largest** common factor of **both** numbers.

Example: The factors of **12** are **1**, **2**, 3, **4**, 6, 12.
The factors of **16** are **1**, **2**, **4**, 8, 16.
The factors they have in **common** are **1**, **2** and **4**.
The **highest common factor** of **12** and **16** is **4**.

Write all the factors of these numbers, highlight the common ones and then identify the highest.

3 Factors of 8: ______________________
Factors of 20: ______________________
The highest common factor of 8 and 20 is: __________

4 Factors of 14: ______________________
Factors of 29: ______________________
The highest common factor of 14 and 29 is: __________

5 Factors of 16: ______________________
Factors of 28: ______________________
The highest common factor of 16 and 28 is: __________

ISBN: 9780170447010

Mixing it up

1 Penny has 36 mints, 30 milkshakes and 48 toffees. She wants to use all of these to make up bags which must each contain the same number of each type of lolly. Find the maximum number of bags she can make, and write down the number of each type of lolly that will be in each.

____

2 a Mac's class is running the hotdog stall at the fair. They do not want any food left over. Sausages come in packs of 12, there are 20 slices in a loaf of bread, and one bottle of sauce will do 25 hot dogs. On past experience, they know they should sell between 200 and 400 hotdogs. How many hotdogs should they buy ingredients for?

____

b How many of each of the following will they need?

Packets of sausages: ______ Loaves of bread: ______ Bottles of sauce: ______

3 Charlie has a piece of card that is 24 cm long and 18 cm wide. He needs to cut it into squares of equal sizes, and use up all the card. If he wants to make each square as big as possible, how many squares would he make and how big would each square be?

____

4 The cathedral bells toll every 8 seconds. The nearby church bells toll every 6 seconds. They both start to toll their bells at exactly 10 am.

a When will their bells first toll at exactly the same time?

____

b Both sets of bells toll for 5 minutes. How many times will their bells toll at the same instant?

____

c What time will it be when they last toll at the same instant?

____

5 The base for our number system is 10. The base for the Babylonian number system was 60, and we have retained 60 for measuring units of time. Based on your knowledge of factors and multiples, what would the advantage be for using 60 as a base for a number system?

____

____

ISBN: 9780170447010

Prime numbers

- A prime number has **exactly two factors**: 1 and itself.

Examples: 2 **is** a prime number because it has exactly **two** factors: **1** and **2**.
7 **is** a prime number because it has exactly **two** factors: **1** and **7**.
6 **is not** a prime number because it has **four** factors: **1**, **2**, **3** and **6**.

Note: 1 **is not** a prime number because it has only **one** factor: **1**.

1 Highlight the prime numbers between 1 and 50. (Hint: You should find fifteen.) This will be useful for the exercise below.

1	2	3	4	5	6	7	8	9	10
11	12	13	14	15	16	17	18	19	20
21	22	23	24	25	26	27	28	29	30
31	32	33	34	35	36	37	38	39	40
41	42	43	44	45	46	47	48	49	50

2 **a** Show calculations to prove that 23 is a prime number.

____

____

____

____

b Is 53 a prime number? Show your reasoning.

____

____

c Fill in the gaps in the following description of what you need to do in order to demonstrate that a number is prime. Words to use:

root **prime** **square** **divide**

I need to ____________ the number by every ____________ number which is less than the ____________ ____________ of the number. If any answers are integers, then the number **is/is not** prime.

 ISBN: 9780170447010

Prime factors

- All non-prime numbers can be written as products of prime factors.
- Prime numbers and their factors are very important in cryptography (writing and using codes), especially for use in cyber security.

Examples:

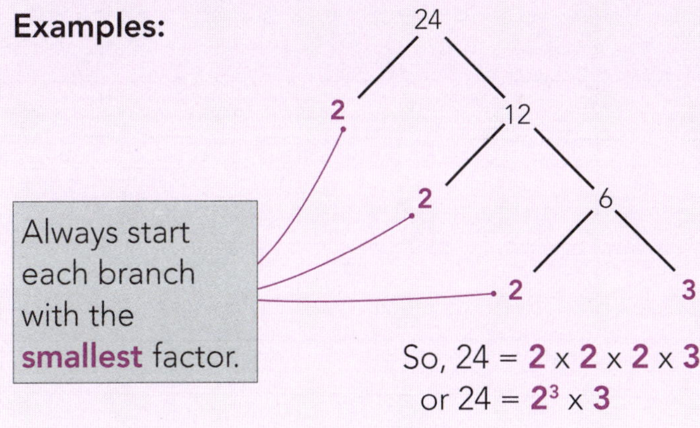

So, 24 = **2** x **2** x **2** x **3**
or 24 = $\mathbf{2^3}$ x **3**

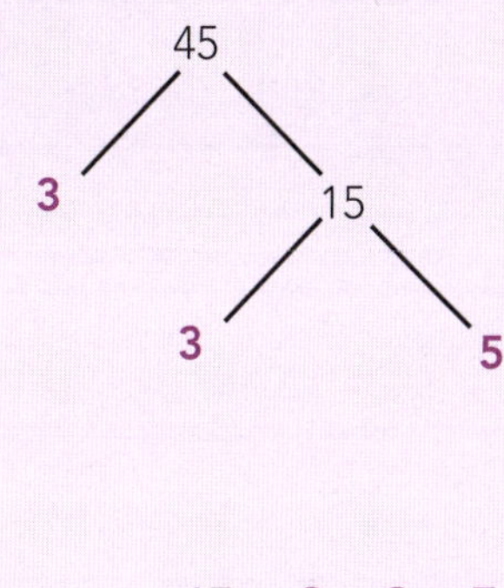

45 = **3** x **3** x **5**
or 45 = $\mathbf{3^2}$ x **5**

Complete these prime factor trees.

3

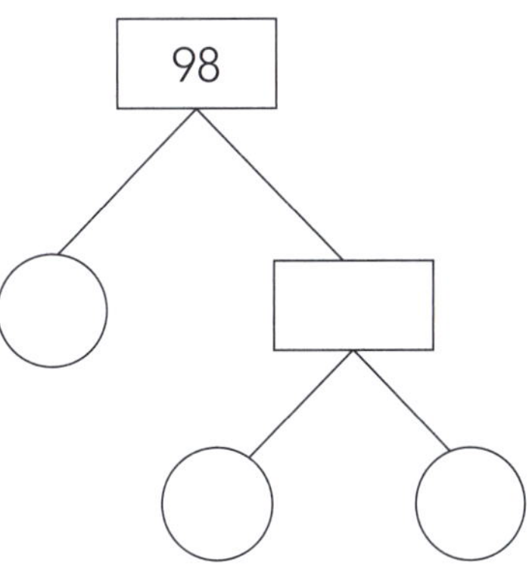

98 = ____________________

4

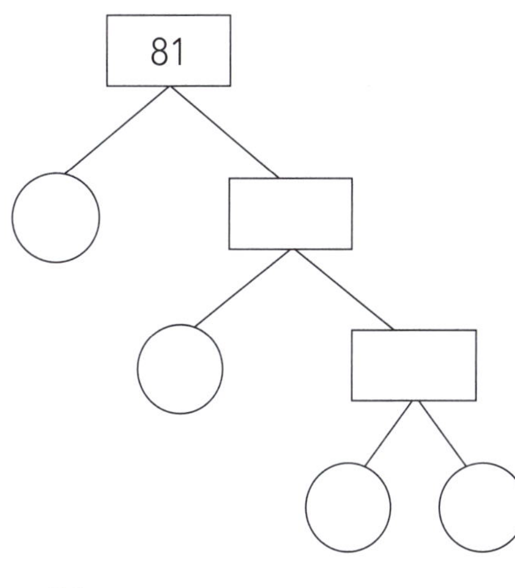

81 = ____________________

Draw factor trees, and use them to help you write these numbers as products of prime factors

5 90 = ____________________

6 72 = ____________________

ISBN: 9780170447010

Investigation

Complete the table.

1

			Prime?
$2^2 - 1$	$4 - 1$	3	✓
$2^3 - 1$			
$2^4 - 1$			
$2^5 - 1$			
$2^6 - 1$			
$2^7 - 1$			
$2^8 - 1$			

Prime numbers that can be written as **$2^n - 1$** are known as **Mersenne** primes. Many prime numbers take this form.

2 Write the value of $2^{12} - 1$, and give a reason why it is *not* a Mersenne prime.

____

3 The next Mersenne prime number is $2^{13} - 1$. What is its value? ______________

4 Another Mersenne prime number is $2^{31} - 1$. What is its value? ______________

5 A new Mersenne prime number was found in August 2019. Its value is $2^{82\,589\,933} - 1$, and it has 24 862 048 digits.

Assume a person can hand write two digits per second.
If a person wrote at that rate continuously, calculate how many days it would take to write out all the digits of this new prime number. Show your calculations.

____

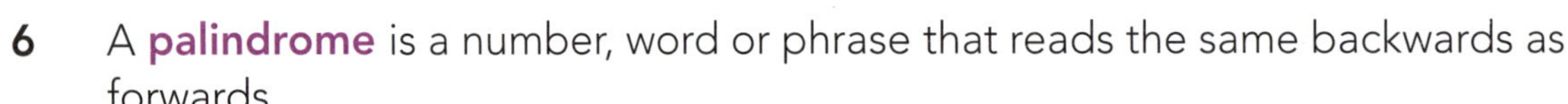

6 A **palindrome** is a number, word or phrase that reads the same backwards as forwards.

Examples: 5, 9009, 123454321, madam, racecar, was it a car or a cat I saw.

Write down the first 10 palindromic prime numbers.

____

 ISBN: 9780170447010

Square numbers

- A square number is a product (x) of two equal counting numbers (counting numbers are 1, 2, 3 …).
- They are written as (number)^2, and we say '(number) **squared**'.
- Square numbers can be drawn as a square pattern of dots.

Draw dots in order to complete the pattern, and fill in the missing numbers:

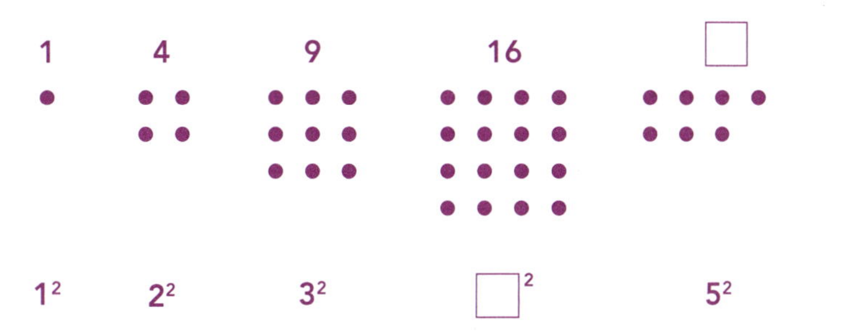

Examples: 81 **is** a square number because it is a product of 9 and 9, and it equals 9^2.
8 **is not** a square number because it cannot be written as a product of two equal numbers. Nor can 8 dots be drawn in a square.

Answer the following.

1 List the square numbers between 30 and 200: ____________________

____

2 The digits of 25 add to 7. Write down two square numbers whose digits add to 16.

____

3 Use prime factorisation to show that 36 is a square number.

____

4 Explain how the prime factorisation of 81 shows that it is a square number.

____

____

5 Use prime factorisation to find out whether 576 is a square number.

____

6 Ana said, 'The square of a whole number is bigger than the original number.' Decide whether her statement is always, sometimes or never true. Explain your answer.

____

____

ISBN: 9780170447010

Cubic numbers

- A cubic number is a product (x) of three equal counting numbers (counting numbers are 1, 2, 3 …).
- They are written as n^3 and we say 'n **cubed**'.
- Positive cubic numbers can be thought of as the volumes of cubes with sides that are counting numbers.

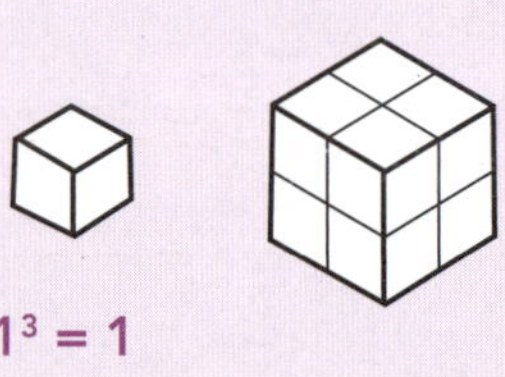
$1^3 = 1$

$2^3 = 8$

$3^3 = 27$

$4^3 = 64$

$5^3 = 125$

Examples: 8 000 **is** a cubic number because it is the product of three equal integers: 20 x 20 x 20, or 20^3.

9 **is not** a cubic number because it cannot be written as a product of three equal integers. Nor can 9 be the volume of a cube with integral sides.

Answer the following.

1 List the next three cubic numbers after 125: ______________________

2 Matiu is making a large cube consisting of layers of different-coloured small cubes. All the small cubes are the same size as the central purple one, and the cubes in each layer are the same colour.

a Complete the table below to show the calculations required to find the number of additional cubes needed to complete each layer.

Layer	Number of extra cubes needed	Total
Core (dark purple)	1	1
1 (light purple)	3^3 – ______ = ______	27
2	______ – 27 = ______	
3	______ – ______ = ______	
4	______ – ______ = ______	

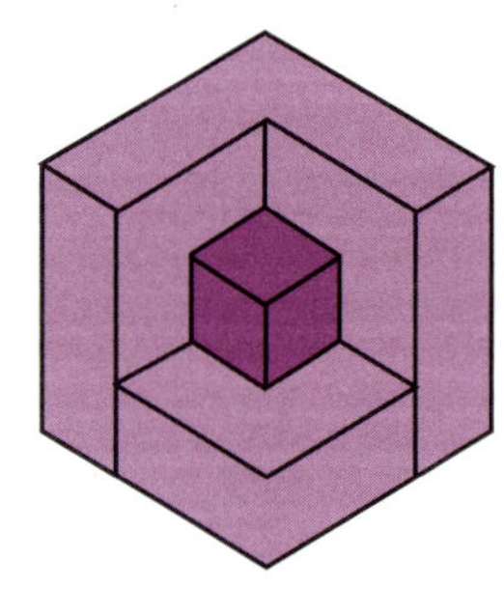

b If he has 1 000 cubes of each colour, calculate the maximum number of layers he can make.

____

____

  ISBN: 9780170447010

Triangular numbers

- A triangular number can be written as the sum of ordered counting numbers, starting from 1.
- Triangular numbers can be thought of as the number of dots needed to complete a triangular pattern.

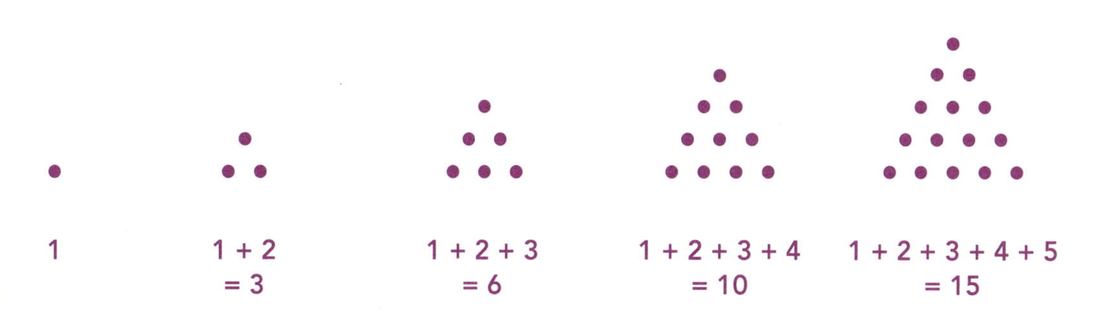

- The first five triangular numbers are **1**, **3**, **6**, **10** and **15**.

Examples: 45 **is** a triangular number because it can be written as:
45 = 1 + 2 + 3 + 4 + 5 + 6 + 7 + 8 + 9

12 **is not** a triangular number because it cannot be written as a sum of ordered counting numbers starting from 1: $12 \neq 1 + 2 + 3 + 4 + \ldots$
Nor can 12 be drawn as a triangle of dots.

Answer the following.

1 List the next six triangular numbers after 15: ____________________

2 Write down two numbers that are both square and triangular numbers: ____________

3 Are there any numbers less than 100 that are both triangular and cubic?

____

4 List five triangular numbers that are palindromes: ____________________

5 **a** What happens if you add any two adjacent triangular numbers?

____

b Use the space below to draw some diagrams that show why this is true.
Hint: Draw your triangular numbers as right-angled triangles:

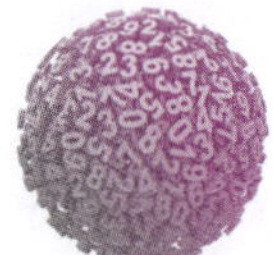

Weird stuff

1 Complete the table below.

Row	Sum of the cubes			Square of the sums		
1	1^3	1	**1**	1^2	1^2	**1**
2	$1^3 + 2^3$	1 + 8	**9**	$(1 + 2)^2$	3^2	**9**
3	$1^3 + 2^3 + 3^3$	1 + 8 + 27	**36**	$(1 + 2 + 3)^2$	6^2	**36**
4						
5						
6						

Proving that $1^3 + 2^3 + 3^3 + \ldots = (1 + 2 + 3 + \ldots)^2$ is not easy, but you can find a visual demonstration at https://en.wikipedia.org/wiki/Squared_triangular_number.

2 **a** Complete the table.

	First	Next 2	Next 3	Next 4	Next 5
Odd numbers	1	3 5	7 9 11	13 15 17 19	21 23 25 27 29
Sum	1	8			
	1^3	2^3			
Mean	1	4			
	1^2	2^2			

b Explain why the sum of each group of odd numbers is a cubic number.

___

___

___

 ISBN: 9780170447010

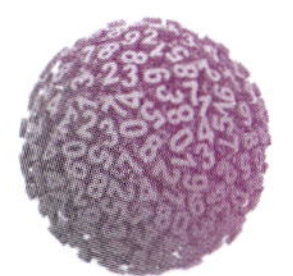

Factorials

- Five students (Arnie, Bertie, Charlie, Danny and Eric) are running a race. In how many different orders can they cross the finish line?

  Any of the five can cross first, so the number of possibilities for first place = 5

  Suppose Arnie comes first. There are four students left, so the number of possibilities for second place = 4

  If Bertie comes second, there are three students left, so the number of possibilities for third place = 3

  Let's say Charlie comes third. There are two students left, so the number of possibilities for fourth place = 2

  If Danny comes fourth, that leaves Eric, so the number of possibilities for fifth place = 1

  This means that the total number of different orders that the five students can cross the line = 5 x 4 x 3 x 2 x 1 = 120.
- We call 5 x 4 x 3 x 2 x 1 'five factorial' and it is written as '5!'.
- Factorials are very useful when calculating probabilities.
- Factorials get very big, very fast, e.g. 13! = 6 227 020 800.
- There will be a button on your calculator for working these out.

  It may look like  or you may have to use .

Examples: **1** Use your calculator to find 7 x 6 x 5 x 4 x 3 x 2 x 1: ________

2 Locate the factorial button on your calculator and use it to find 7!: ________

Write the following factorials in full, and calculate their values.

1 4! = ____________________

= ____________________

2 6! = ____________________

= ____________________

3 6 x 5! = ____________________

= ____________________

4 What do you notice about your last two answers?

____

Use the factorial button on your calculator to answer the following.

5 $9(4! + 6!) =$ ____________________

6 $(7! - 5!)^2 \div 6! =$ ____________________

ISBN: 9780170447010

Powers

Powers are used to indicate how many times a number (the base) is multiplied by itself.

The **10** is called the **base**.

The **4** is known as the **power** or the **exponent** or the **index**.

Example: $10^4 = 10 \times 10 \times 10 \times 10$
$= 10\,000$

Important: **anything^1 = itself** e.g. $27^1 = 27$
anything^0 = 1 e.g. $27^0 = 1$

The power indicates how many times you need to multiply.

The brackets are important. Compare the two answers.

Examples: $-(3^4) = -3 \times 3 \times 3 \times 3$
$= -81$

$(-3)^4 = -3 \times -3 \times -3 \times -3$
$= 81$

Finding powers on your calculator

- Powers of numbers can get really big, so knowing how to find them on your calculator is **very** useful.

For squares: use a button that looks like this:  e.g. show that $14^2 = 196$.

For cubes: use a button that looks like this:  e.g. show that $7^3 = 343$.

For all other powers: use a button that looks like this:  or  or ^
e.g. show that $3^9 = 19\,683$.

Write the following as powers.

1 $7 \times 7 \times 7 \times 7 =$ ______________

2 $-6 \times 6 \times 6 =$ ______________

3 $-8 \times -8 \times -8 \times -8 =$ ______________

4 $-10 \times -10 \times -10 \times -10 \times -10 =$ ______________

Without using your calculator, find the values of the following.

5 $10^5 =$ ______________

6 $8^0 =$ ______________

7 $(0.5)^2 =$ ______________

8 $(-0.1)^4 =$ ______________

ISBN: 9780170447010

9 $5^3 =$ ______ **10** $-0.5^2 =$ ______

11 $-10^4 =$ ______ **12** $(-10)^4 =$ ______

13 $-9^1 =$ ______ **14** $(-0.3)^0 =$ ______

15 $10^6 =$ ______ **16** $(-0.2)^2 =$ ______

Use your calculator to find the values of the following.

17 $7^5 =$ ______ **18** $17^3 =$ ______

19 $214^2 =$ ______ **20** $-27^4 =$ ______

21 $(-1.3)^6 =$ ______ **22** $0.25^3 =$ ______

23 $(0.01)^2 =$ ______ **24** $0.95^4 =$ ______

Puzzle

Match the answers in the boxes to each of the questions below. Use your calculator to help you. You will not need to use all the answers.

–0.0001	0.01	1	100 000 000	–10 000 000
–1 000 000	–0.01	100 000	–10 000	1 000 000
–100 000 000	–100 000	0.1	10 000 000	–0.001

1 $-10^5 \times 10^3 =$ ______ **2** $0.001 \times 10^3 =$ ______

3 $10^6 \div 0.1 =$ ______ **4** $-10^0 \div 10^4 =$ ______

5 $10^2 \times (-10)^5 =$ ______ **6** $-10^7 \div 10^5 \div 10^5 =$ ______

7 $10^2 \div (-10)^0 \div 10^4 =$ ______ **8** $(-10)^7 \times (-10^3) \div 10^2 =$ ______

9 $10^4 \times (-10)^0 \div 10^5 =$ ______ **10** $10^8 \times 10^1 \div (-10)^5 =$ ______

11 $(-10^5 \div 10^2)^2 =$ ______ **12** $10^{10} \div (-10 \times 10^3)^3 =$ ______

ISBN: 9780170447010

Negative powers

- Complete the following patterns.

10^4	10 000	÷ 10
10^3	1 000	÷ 10
10^2	100	÷ 10
10^1	10	÷ 10
10^0	1	÷ 10
10^{-1}	$0.1 = \frac{1}{10} = \frac{1}{10^1}$	÷ 10
10^{-2}		÷ 10
10^{-3}		

2^4	16	÷ 2
2^3	8	÷ 2
2^2	4	÷ 2
2^1	2	÷ 2
2^0	1	÷ 2
2^{-1}	$\frac{1}{2} = \frac{1}{2^1}$	÷ 2
2^{-2}		÷ 2
2^{-3}		

- In general terms: $\mathbf{a^{-b} = \frac{1}{a^b}}$

Examples: **1** $5^{-2} = \frac{1}{25} = 0.04$ **2** $(0.2)^{-4} = \frac{1}{(0.2)^4} = 625$

Evaluate the following. Write your answers as fractions.

1 $7^{-2} =$ ________________ **2** $10^{-3} =$ ________________

3 $3^{-4} =$ ________________ **4** $8^{-1} =$ ________________

Evaluate the following. Write your answers as decimals or whole numbers.

5 $5^{-2} =$ ________________ **6** $10^{-4} =$ ________________

7 $2^{-3} =$ ________________ **8** $4^{-1} =$ ________________

9 $(0.1)^{-2} =$ ________________ **10** $\left(\frac{1}{2}\right)^{-3} =$ ________________

ISBN: 9780170447010

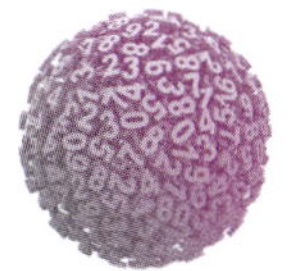

Roots

- Finding a root is the opposite of finding a power.
- The **square root** is written as $\sqrt{\ }$. You do not need to write $\sqrt[2]{\ }$.

  e.g. $\sqrt{49} = \sqrt{7 \times 7}$
  $= 7$
- The **cube root** is written as $\sqrt[3]{\ }$.

  e.g. $\sqrt[3]{64} = \sqrt[3]{4 \times 4 \times 4}$
  $= 4$
- The **fourth root** is written $\sqrt[4]{\ }$, the **fifth root** is written as $\sqrt[5]{\ }$, etc.

  e.g. $\sqrt[4]{81} = \sqrt[4]{3 \times 3 \times 3 \times 3}$
  $= 3$

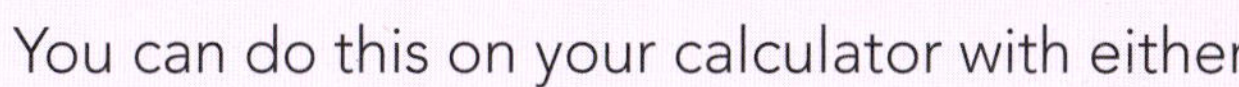

You can do this on your calculator with either 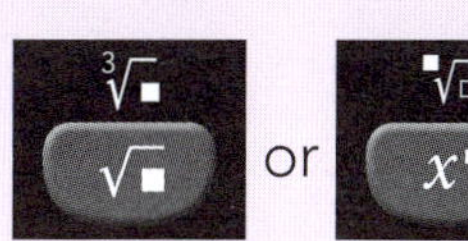 or $x^{\blacksquare}$.

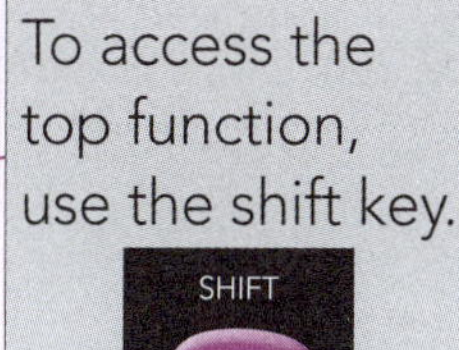

To access the top function, use the shift key.

Without using your calculator, find the following roots.

1 $\sqrt{81} =$ ______________________

2 $\sqrt[3]{125} =$ ______________________

3 $\sqrt[5]{-32} =$ ______________________

4 $\sqrt[2]{1\,000\,000} =$ ______________________

5 $\sqrt[7]{128} =$ ______________________

6 $\sqrt[4]{625} =$ ______________________

7 $\sqrt[9]{-1} =$ ______________________

8 $\sqrt[7]{-10\,000\,000} =$ ______________________

Use your calculator to find the values of the following.

9 $\sqrt{0.25} =$ ______________________

10 $\sqrt{15\,129} =$ ______________________

11 $\sqrt[3]{0.002744} =$ ______________________

12 $\sqrt[5]{-7776} =$ ______________________

13 $\sqrt[4]{39.0625} =$ ______________________

14 $\sqrt[8]{10^{-8}} =$ ______________________

15 $\sqrt[3]{6^2 + 180} =$ ______________________

16 $\sqrt[4]{10^3 - 744} =$ ______________________

ISBN: 9780170447010

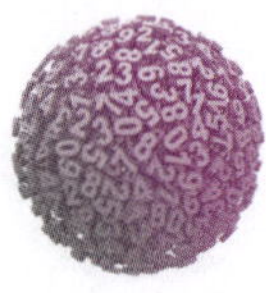

Mixing it up

1 $3^2 \times 3^3$ = ____________ **2** 3^5 = ____________

3 Are your last two answers the same? ____________

What number should go in the box: $3^2 \times 3^3 = 3^{\square}$? ____________

4 $\frac{2^7}{2^3}$ = ____________ **5** 2^4 = ____________

6 Are your last two answers the same? ____________

What number should go in the box: $\frac{2^7}{2^3} = 2^{\square}$? ____________

7 $(2^3)^4$ = ____________ **8** 2^{12} = ____________

9 Are your last two answers the same? ____________

What number should go in the box: $(2^3)^4 = 2^{\square}$? ____________

Write the following answers as powers.

10 $2^5 \times 2^7$ = ____________ **11** $5^{10} \div 5^2$ = ____________

12 $(11^2)^3$ = ____________ **13** $(0.6)^7 \div (-0.6)^2$ = ____________

14 $-2 \times 2^7 \times 2^4$ = ____________ **15** $((0.1)^4)^2$ = ____________

16 $(5^2)^{-1}$ = ____________ **17** $3^{-4} \times 3^2 \times 3^5$ = ____________

Use your calculator to work out the following.

18 $2^5 \div 5^{-2}$ = ____________ **19** $18^2 \div 3^4 \times 9^2$ = ____________

20 $10^5 - (3^4)^2$ = ____________ **21** $(0.6)^4 - (0.02)^3$ = ____________

22 $5^{-2} + 0.2^3 + 0.8$ = ____________ **23** $\sqrt{(0.36)^2} + (0.8)^2$ = ____________

24 $\sqrt[3]{0.000027} - 0.1^2$ = ____________ **25** $((13^0) + 5)^3$ = ____________

  ISBN: 9780170447010

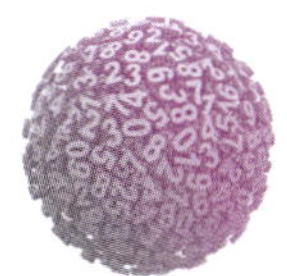

Order of operations

- **BEDMAS** helps us to remember the order of operations.
- If you have several division signs or several multiplication signs, work from left to right.
- The horizontal division symbol in a fraction means you must bracket the numerator and bracket the denominator.

Using BEDMAS, calculate the following. You should be able to do these without a calculator.

1 $\frac{3 + 5^2}{9 - 2} =$ __________

2 $\frac{-2(-5 - 1)^2}{3^2} =$ __________

3 $5(3 - 2^2) + 1 =$ __________

4 $4(3 - 6)^2 \div 12 =$ __________

5 $12 \times -3 + 5^2 - 6 \div -2 =$ __________

6 $36 \div (-3)^2 - 6 \times 2 + 1 =$ __________

7 $\frac{7^2 - 5}{11} - 3 \times 2 =$ __________

8 $6^2 \times 2 - \frac{12 - 4}{2} =$ __________

9 $\frac{-4(2^3 - 5)^2}{\sqrt{64}} =$ __________

10 $\sqrt{\frac{1}{4}} \times \frac{2(5^2 - 3 \times 5)}{5} =$ __________

Use the rules below and the numerals 1, 2, 3, 4, 5 and 6 exactly once to make the totals indicated.

- Use only the symbols +, –, x, ÷, (,), ^ (for 'to the power of') and $\sqrt{\ }$.
- You must use at least one symbol between every digit.
- You may use a symbol before the first digit and after the last.

One solution is given in the answers. If you find a different one, check it with your neighbour.

Example: $(2^3 - 6)^4 + \sqrt{5 - 1} = 14$

11 ____________________ = 12

12 ____________________ = –11

13 ____________________ = 23

14 ____________________ = 13

15 ____________________ = 81

16 ____________________ = 28

ISBN: 9780170447010

Using your calculator

Do the calculations on the next page using your calculator, then turn your calculator upside down and add the word to the story below. Be careful to check that it makes sense.

Example: $3^5 \times 5^2 = 6075$, upside down this spells SLOG.

Arctic adventure

The snow piled high on the 1 ____________ casting 2 ____________ light into the 3 ____________. He would 4 ____________ the blocks of ice stacked like 5 ____________ creating an 6 ____________ of semi-warmth on the ice. The cold crept through the 7 ____________ of his boots, over the Swanndri 8 ____________ on his socks and up his 9 ____________. 10 ____________ was so pleased 11 ____________ had agreed to go too, as doing this 12 ____________ would not be much fun. They were both 13 ____________ for the 14 ____________ scholarship to study the snow 15 ____________ and 16 ____________ had to 17 ____________ 18 ____________ to apply. He wasn't sure this was the 19 ____________ they were promised, alone and cold on this deserted part of the 20 ____________, harsh 21 ____________ making everything hard, and freezing cold. The 22 ____________ on the ice as it sparkled in the sun hid the threat of polar bears that could 23 ____________ them at any time and he hadn't even seen a snow 24 ____________ yet. They would 25 ____________ in their sleeping bags, their heads would 26 ____________, the hot food in their 27 ____________ struggling to warm them. 28 ____________ checked his sleeping bag was tight. A 29 ____________ drawstring and you could freeze to death. He began to 30 ____________ about that and told 31 ____________ to check his. They did not hear the muffled squawk from the 32 ____________ of the snow bird or the slush of the snow under the feet of the 33 ____________ polar bear as it approached.

 ISBN: 9780170447010

1 $\dfrac{15^3 - 289}{\sqrt{0.16}}$

2 $\left(\dfrac{6^3}{2} + 6\right)(18^2 - 7)$

3 $\dfrac{3}{40} + 1.1 \times 10^{-3}$

4 $2^4(243 - \sqrt[3]{512})$

5 $0.7^2\left(\dfrac{10 + 24 \times 5}{100}\right)$

6 $1 + 5^4(2^3 - 2)$

7 $5 \times 10^4 + 38 \times 10^2 - 95$

8 $\dfrac{5 - 0.75 - 1 \times 10^{-3}}{7}$

9 $3(2^3 \times 5(6 \times 2^3 - 1) - 1)$

10 $2^2(\sqrt[3]{2\,197}\,(2^{10} + 9))$

11 $2(10 + 2(100 + 2(10 + 2(1\,920))))$

12 $3\left(\dfrac{9}{13} - \dfrac{5}{26}\right)^2 - 4.5 \times 10^{-2}$

13 $3^3 \times \left((\sqrt{1.96} \times 10^6 + 10^3) - \left(\dfrac{5!}{0.3} + 1\right)\right)$

14 $\dfrac{10^0(5^3 - 11^2 - 1)}{5! - 20}$

15 $\left(\sqrt[9]{512}\right)^3 \times \dfrac{98}{14}(2^9 + 7 \times 17)$

16 $\dfrac{\sqrt[3]{2\,197}}{0.25}\left(\dfrac{3^7 - 121}{2}\right)$

17 $2\dfrac{7}{11}\left(2 + 3\left(\dfrac{10}{0.125}\right)\right)$

18 $20\left(\sqrt[4]{2\,401}\left(16^2 - \dfrac{231}{7}\right)\right)$

19 $587 \times \dfrac{2 \times 4! - 1}{2^{-1}}$

20 $200^2 - \dfrac{13\sqrt{1\,369}}{0.25}$

21 $\dfrac{5.31}{10^{-8}} + 316\sqrt{289}\,(2^7 - 15)$

22 $\dfrac{2^4 \times 7^3}{10^{-1}} + 14^2$

23 $2^5 \times 10^3 + 3^3 \times \sqrt[6]{15\,625}$

24 $23\sqrt[10]{1\,024}\,(6! + 41)$

25 $\dfrac{7! + 32}{\sqrt[3]{4\,096}}$

26 $\dfrac{3 + 2(4 + 5(4 + 5(946)))}{0.125}$

27 $46(8 + 5(4 + 5(8 + 5(923))))$

28 $\dfrac{116}{29} \times \sqrt{169}\,(3^6 + 304)$

29 $3.5 \times 10^4 + \sqrt[4]{2\,401}$

30 $20\sqrt{7\,921}\,(7^3 - 32)$

31 $20(10 \times 3! + 1) + 3.0 \times 10^4$

32 $\dfrac{2}{3} \times 681 \times \sqrt[4]{83\,521}$

33 $3(2 + 2(2 + 2(2 + 2(4!))))$

ISBN: 9780170447010

Words to calculations

Match the calculations with the stories below, and calculate the answer to each. You will not need to use all of these calculations.

$\dfrac{18 - 24 + 3 \times 12}{4}$	$\dfrac{3(18 \times 4 - 12)}{2}$	$\dfrac{24 \times 4}{2} - 18 - 12$
$\dfrac{3 \times 12 - 18}{4} - 2$	$\dfrac{24 - 3 \times 18}{4} - 2$	$24 + \dfrac{3 \times 18}{4} - 2$
$\dfrac{24 \times 4 - 12}{3} - 18$	$\dfrac{3 \times 12 - 18 - 2}{4}$	$\dfrac{12 + 18 + 2 \times 3}{3}$
$\dfrac{3(24 \times 4)}{2} - 12$	$\dfrac{12 + 18 + 12 \times 3}{4}$	$\dfrac{24 - 18 + 3 \times 12}{4}$

	Story	Calculation	Solution
1	Grandma, Dad and two children visited a nature reserve. Grandma had a Gold Card so her ticket was \$12, Dad's cost \$18, and the children were \$3 each. Calculate their average ticket price.		\$ _______
2	At the fair, Mick and his two brothers had to pay a total of \$12 for a stall, from which they sold 24 bags of cones for \$4 per bag. They shared their profit equally, but Mick spent \$18 at other stalls. How much more or less did he have at the end of the day?		\$ _______
3	Henare was raising money for a school trip. He hired a \$12 stand at the fair, and sold 18 plants for \$4 each. His dad said he would add half of the amount that Henare earned. How much did Henare raise, including his dad's contribution?		\$ _______
4	Milly has \$18, but she owes her dad \$24. She weeded the garden for three hours, for which she was paid \$12 per hour. She repaid her dad, and then spent all her money on presents of equal value for her four friends. How much was each present?		\$ _______
5	Ruby worked for three hours at the local bookshop where she is paid \$18 per hour. On the way home she spent three-quarters of her earnings on a shirt. Then her bus fare cost \$2. If Ruby started the day with \$24 in her purse, how much did she have at the end of the day?		\$ _______
6	There were three dozen eggs left at camp. The teacher dropped two eggs, and 18 people ate a boiled egg for breakfast. The remaining eggs were used to make four quiches. On average, how many eggs were used in each quiche?		_______

ISBN: 9780170447010

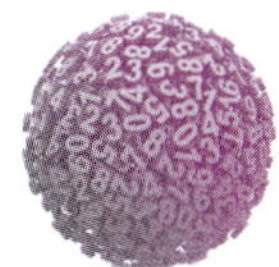

Fractions

- Fractions are a way of writing numbers or parts of numbers.

Numerators and denominators

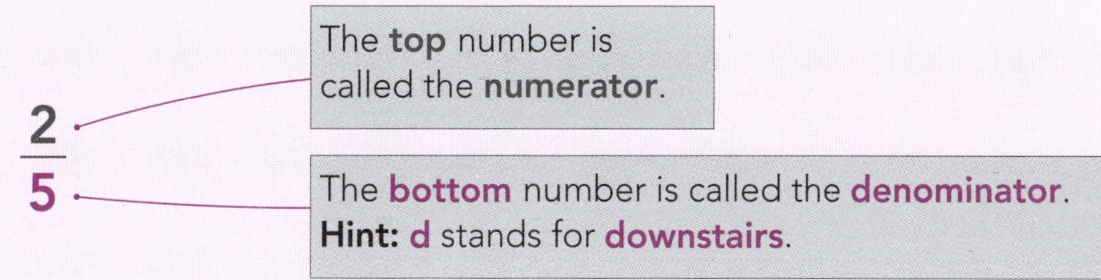

Shade the fraction represented in each diagram and cross out the word to make a true statement.

1

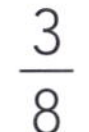

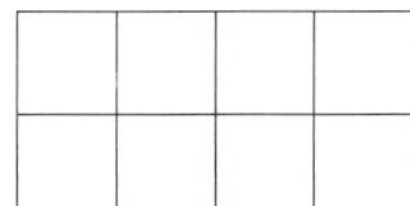

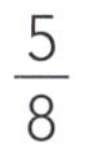

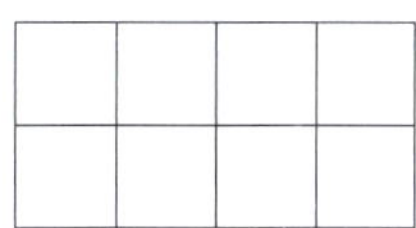

When the **numerator** increases, the size of the shaded section **increases/decreases**.

2

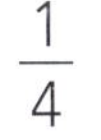

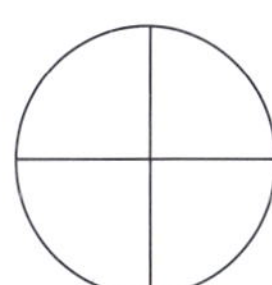

$\frac{1}{6}$

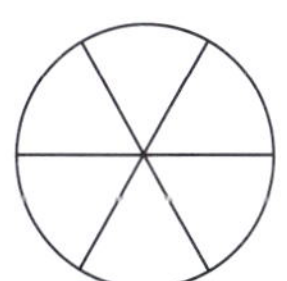

When the **denominator** increases, the size of the shaded section **increases/decreases**.

3 Place these fractions in the correct ascending order (smallest to largest).

$\frac{1}{17}$ $\frac{12}{17}$ $\frac{5}{17}$ $\frac{11}{17}$ $\frac{15}{17}$ $\frac{20}{17}$ $\frac{2}{17}$

		$\frac{5}{17}$				

4 Place these fractions in the correct ascending order (smallest to largest).

$\frac{3}{10}$ $\frac{3}{7}$ $\frac{3}{4}$ $\frac{3}{5}$ $\frac{3}{13}$ $\frac{3}{11}$ $\frac{3}{17}$

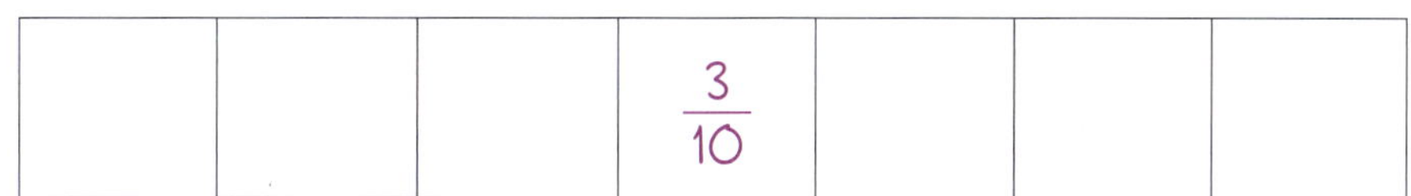

ISBN: 9780170447010

Equivalent fractions

- Equivalent fractions are fractions that are written with different denominators, but which have the same value.

$$\frac{2}{3} = \frac{8}{12}$$

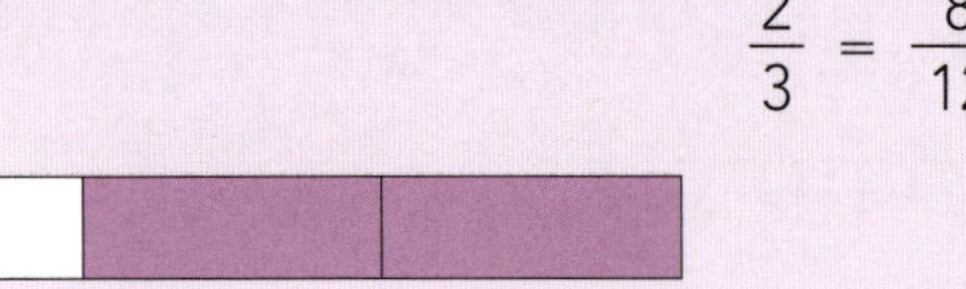

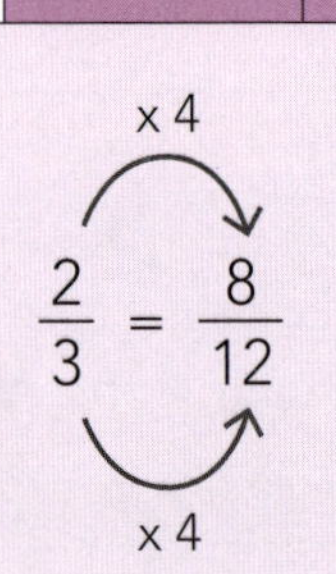

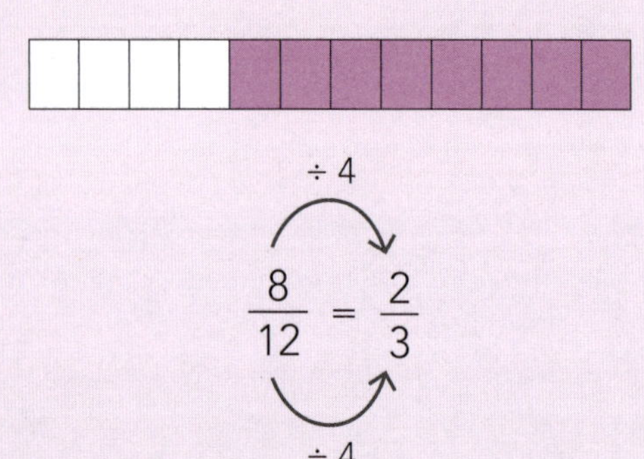

Fill in the gaps to create equivalent fractions.

1 $\frac{3}{24} = \frac{1}{\_\_}$

2 $\frac{4}{5} = \frac{\_\_}{15}$

3 $\frac{15}{24} = \frac{\_\_}{8}$

4 $\frac{6}{21} = \frac{2}{\_\_}$

5 $\frac{2}{3} = \frac{\_\_}{27}$

Write each fraction in its simplest form.

6 $\frac{9}{15} =$

7 $\frac{20}{24} =$

8 $\frac{12}{32} =$

9 $\frac{27}{30} =$

10 $\frac{35}{60} =$

Find the missing values to make all fractions equivalent.

11 $\frac{14}{21} = \frac{\_\_}{60} = \frac{18}{\_\_} = \frac{\_\_}{63} = \frac{80}{\_\_} = \frac{\_\_}{3} = \frac{24}{\_\_}$

12 $\frac{27}{45} = \frac{\_\_}{20} = \frac{36}{\_\_} = \frac{\_\_}{25} = \frac{3}{\_\_} = \frac{\_\_}{90} = \frac{18}{\_\_}$

13 $\frac{15}{24} = \frac{\_\_}{96} = \frac{5}{\_\_} = \frac{20}{\_\_} = \frac{\_\_}{16} = \frac{125}{\_\_} = \frac{\_\_}{40}$

  ISBN: 9780170447010

Converting between improper and mixed fractions

- An **improper** fraction is when the numerator is bigger than the denominator.

Example: $\frac{9}{4}$

- A **mixed** fraction is a combination of a whole number and a fraction.

Example: $2\frac{1}{4}$

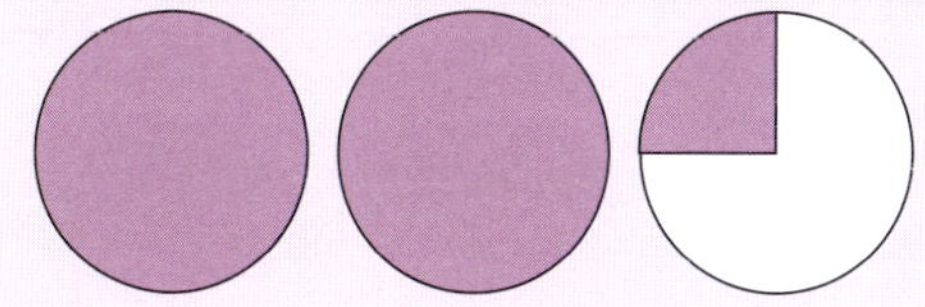

Complete the table. The first one has been done for you.

	Improper fraction	Mixed fraction
1	$\frac{19}{9}$ Nineteen ninths	$2\frac{1}{9}$ Two and one ninth
2	____ ____________	____ ____________
3	____ ____________	____ ____________
4	____ ____________	____ ____________

ISBN: 9780170447010

Converting improper fractions to mixed fractions

Example: Convert $\frac{25}{9}$ into a mixed fraction.

$$\frac{25}{9} = \frac{9}{9} + \frac{9}{9} + \frac{7}{9}$$

$$= \mathbf{2}\frac{\mathbf{7}}{9}$$

Remember, $\frac{9}{9} = 1$.

There are **2** lots of 9 in 25, with **7** ninths left over.

Complete the following.

5 $\frac{19}{7} = \frac{7}{7} + \frac{7}{7} + \frac{\square}{7} = 2\frac{\square}{7}$

6 $\frac{14}{3} = \frac{3}{3} + \frac{3}{3} + \frac{3}{3} + \frac{3}{3} + \frac{\square}{3} = \square\frac{\square}{3}$

7 $\frac{31}{6} = 5\frac{\square}{6}$

8 $\frac{29}{8} = \square\frac{5}{8}$

9 $\frac{11}{4} =$

10 $\frac{20}{9} =$

11 $\frac{33}{5} =$

12 $\frac{28}{11} =$

13 $\frac{52}{7} =$

14 $\frac{143}{25} =$

Converting mixed fractions to improper fractions

Example: Convert $3\frac{4}{7}$ into an improper fraction.

$$3\frac{4}{7} = \frac{\mathbf{7}}{7} + \frac{\mathbf{7}}{7} + \frac{\mathbf{7}}{7} + \frac{\mathbf{4}}{7}$$

$$= \frac{\mathbf{25}}{7}$$

There are **3** lots of **7** sevenths (**21** sevenths), with **4** sevenths left over.

Complete the following.

15 $3\frac{2}{9} = \frac{9}{9} + \frac{9}{9} + \frac{9}{9} + \frac{2}{9} = \frac{\square}{9}$

16 $1\frac{13}{15} = \frac{15}{15} + \frac{13}{15} = \frac{\square}{15}$

17 $2\frac{3}{11} = \frac{\square}{11}$

18 $5\frac{3}{7} = \frac{\square}{7}$

19 $11\frac{1}{4} =$

20 $2\frac{5}{6} =$

21 $3\frac{9}{20} =$

22 $12\frac{1}{4} =$

ISBN: 9780170447010

Adding and subtracting fractions

With the same denominators

- To add or subtract fractions with the **same denominator**, you add or subtract the numerator. The denominator does not change.

Example: $\frac{\mathbf{1}}{8} + \frac{\mathbf{3}}{8} = \frac{\mathbf{4}}{8} = \frac{1}{2}$

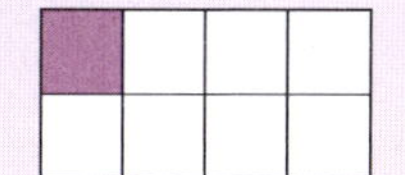 + 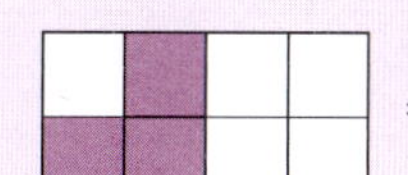 = 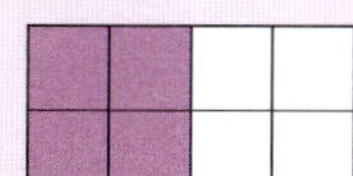

The denominator remains an 8.

With different denominators

- To add or subtract fractions with a **different denominator**, you must first change the **denominator(s)** so that they are the **same**.

Example:

1 $\frac{3}{8} + \frac{1}{2} = \frac{3}{8} + \left(\frac{1}{2} \times \frac{4}{4}\right)$

$= \frac{\mathbf{3}}{8} + \frac{\mathbf{4}}{8}$

$= \frac{\mathbf{7}}{8}$

This denominator needs to become 8.

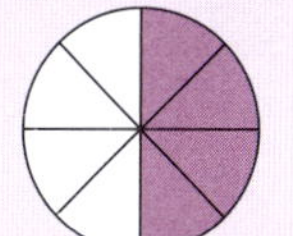 + 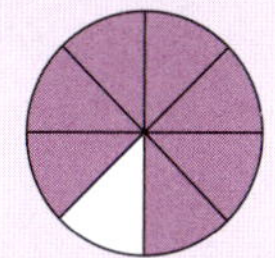

Because the denominators are the same, we can add the numerators.

2 $\frac{2}{3} - \frac{1}{4} = \left(\frac{2}{3} \times \frac{4}{4}\right) - \left(\frac{1}{4} \times \frac{3}{3}\right)$

$= \frac{8}{\mathbf{12}} - \frac{3}{\mathbf{12}}$

$= \frac{5}{\mathbf{12}}$

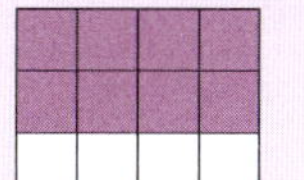 − 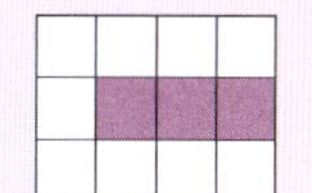 = 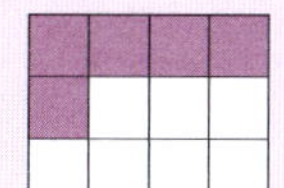

We need to change both denominators. The easiest way to do this is to multiply by each other.

12 is called a **common denominator** because it is the same for both fractions.

Add or subtract these fractions. Where possible, write your answers as mixed fractions.

1 $\frac{2}{7} + \frac{3}{7} =$ ______________________

$=$ ______________________

2 $\frac{3}{4} + \frac{1}{8} =$ ______________________

$=$ ______________________

3 $\frac{1}{6} + \frac{2}{3} =$ ______________________

$=$ ______________________

4 $\frac{5}{9} - \frac{1}{2} =$ ______________________

$=$ ______________________

5 $\frac{4}{7} - \frac{1}{5} =$ ____________

= ____________

6 $\frac{4}{7} + \frac{1}{4} =$ ____________

= ____________

7 $\frac{7}{10} + \frac{3}{4} =$ ____________

= ____________

8 $\frac{7}{8} - \frac{3}{7} =$ ____________

= ____________

9 $\frac{7}{11} + \frac{3}{4} =$ ____________

= ____________

10 $\frac{5}{12} + \frac{4}{5} =$ ____________

= ____________

11 $\frac{13}{25} + 1\frac{9}{20} =$ ____________

= ____________

12 $\frac{9}{11} + 2\frac{1}{4} =$ ____________

= ____________

Mixing it up

1 There are 4 000 species of cockroach, of which 20 are classified as pests. What fraction of cockroach species are classified as not being pests?

____

2 'Eighteen-carat gold' is made of a mixture of 18 parts of gold with 6 parts of other metals, which are added to make it harder. What fraction of 18-carat gold is other metals?

____

3 In a recent study it was established that in the average human adult body, there are about 70 trillion cells. Of these, 40 trillion are bacterial cells. What fraction of the number of cells in the average human body is human cells?

____

4 The largest organ in the human body is the skin, which makes up $\frac{3}{20}$ of its total mass. The liver and brain are next in size, and they each make up $\frac{1}{20}$.

What fraction of the mass of the body is not made up of skin, liver or brain?

____

ISBN: 9780170447010

Multiplying fractions

- To multiply fractions, **multiply the numerators** and then **multiply the denominators**.
- Mixed fractions must be converted to improper fractions first.
- If possible, simplify the answer and write it as a mixed fraction.

Examples:

1 $\frac{5}{6} \times \frac{3}{7} = \frac{5 \times 3}{6 \times 7}$

$= \frac{15}{42}$ ← Simplify.

$= \frac{5}{14}$

2 $2\frac{3}{4} \times 1\frac{2}{5} = \frac{11}{4} \times \frac{7}{5}$ ← First convert mixed fractions to improper fractions.

$= \frac{11 \times 7}{4 \times 5}$

$= \frac{77}{20}$

$= 3\frac{17}{20}$ ← Then convert back to a mixed fraction.

Multiply these fractions and simplify when possible.

1 $\frac{2}{3} \times \frac{4}{5} =$ ____________

$=$ ____________

2 $\frac{5}{6} \times \frac{2}{3} =$ ____________

$=$ ____________

3 $\frac{1}{4} \times \frac{2}{3} \times \frac{5}{6} =$ ____________

$=$ ____________

$=$ ____________

4 $\frac{4}{11} \times 1\frac{1}{2} =$ ____________

$=$ ____________

$=$ ____________

5 $1\frac{1}{3} \times 2\frac{1}{2} =$ ____________

$=$ ____________

$=$ ____________

6 $1\frac{3}{5} \times 1\frac{5}{8} =$ ____________

$=$ ____________

$=$ ____________

7 $5\frac{3}{4} \times 2\frac{1}{7} =$ ____________

$=$ ____________

$=$ ____________

8 $8\frac{1}{4} \times 5\frac{1}{2} =$ ____________

$=$ ____________

$=$ ____________

9 $1\frac{1}{3} \times 2\frac{1}{2} \times \frac{1}{2} =$ ____________

$=$ ____________

$=$ ____________

10 $3\frac{9}{10} \times 1\frac{1}{2} \times 2\frac{3}{5} =$ ____________

$=$ ____________

$=$ ____________

ISBN: 9780170447010

Dividing fractions

Reciprocals

The **reciprocal** of the fraction $\frac{a}{b}$ is $\frac{b}{a}$.

- You may like to think of this as 'turning the fraction upside down'.
- To find the reciprocal of a mixed fraction, you must convert it to an improper fraction first.

Examples:

1 The reciprocal of $\frac{9}{11}$ is $\frac{11}{9}$.

2 $5\frac{7}{8} = \frac{47}{8}$, so the reciprocal of $5\frac{7}{8}$ is $\frac{8}{47}$.

3 $5 = \frac{5}{1}$, so the reciprocal of 5 is $\frac{1}{5}$.

Write reciprocals of the following numbers.

1 $\frac{6}{13}$ Reciprocal = ____________

2 $\frac{17}{25}$ Reciprocal = ____________

3 $2\frac{5}{6}$ Reciprocal = ____________

4 $9\frac{2}{7}$ Reciprocal = ____________

5 37 Reciprocal = ____________

6 $105\frac{2}{3}$ Reciprocal = ____________

To divide fractions

- Mixed fractions must be converted to improper fractions first.
- Trick to dividing fractions:
  1 Leave the first fraction unchanged.
  2 Write the reciprocal of the second fraction.
  3 Multiply the two together.

If possible, simplify the answer and write it as a mixed fraction.

Examples:

1

$$\frac{4}{5} \div \frac{2}{3} = \frac{4}{5} \times \frac{3}{2}$$

Multiply by the reciprocal of the second fraction.

$$= \frac{4 \times 3}{5 \times 2}$$

Multiply instead of divide.

$$= \frac{12}{10}$$

$$= \frac{6}{5}$$

Simplify.

$$= 1\frac{1}{5}$$

Change to a mixed fraction.

ISBN: 9780170447010

2 $5\frac{1}{4} \div 3\frac{1}{2} = \frac{21}{4} \div \frac{7}{2}$ — Turn both mixed fractions into improper fractions.

$= \frac{21}{4} \times \frac{2}{7}$ — Multiply by the reciprocal of the second fraction.

$= \frac{42}{28}$ — Divide the numerator and the denominator by the HCF – in this case 14.

$= \frac{3}{2}$

Divide these fractions and simplify when possible. Where appropriate, write your answers as mixed fractions.

7 $\frac{1}{4} \div \frac{3}{7} =$ __________
$=$ __________
$=$ __________

8 $\frac{1}{3} \div \frac{1}{6} =$ __________
$=$ __________
$=$ __________

9 $\frac{3}{4} \div \frac{5}{12} =$ __________
$=$ __________
$=$ __________

10 $\frac{2}{3} \div \frac{4}{9} =$ __________
$=$ __________
$=$ __________

11 $\frac{8}{9} \div 1\frac{1}{3} =$ __________
$=$ __________
$=$ __________

12 $4\frac{4}{7} \div \frac{8}{21} =$ __________
$=$ __________
$=$ __________

13 $2\frac{4}{5} \div 1\frac{13}{15} =$ __________
$=$ __________
$=$ __________

14 $2\frac{5}{8} \times \frac{2}{3} \div 1\frac{3}{4} =$ __________
$=$ __________
$=$ __________

15 $2\frac{4}{9} \div 1\frac{1}{3} \times \frac{5}{11} =$ __________
$=$ __________
$=$ __________

16 $3 \div 1\frac{1}{5} \div 1\frac{1}{4} =$ __________
$=$ __________
$=$ __________

ISBN: 9780170447010

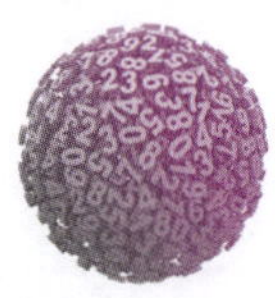

Challenge 1

1 **a** The school council has been given $3\frac{1}{2}$ watermelons, which they will cut up and sell during the gala sports. If each piece is $\frac{1}{24}$ of a melon, how many pieces will they have for sale?

____

b They sell $\frac{3}{4}$ of the pieces by 3 pm, and give the rest away. What fraction of a watermelon did they give away?

____

c Of the watermelon pieces that were sold, $\frac{1}{9}$ were sold to staff. What fraction of a melon did the staff consume?

____

Combining roots and fractions

$$\sqrt{\frac{a^2}{b^2}} = \frac{\sqrt{a^2}}{\sqrt{b^2}} = \frac{a}{b}$$

Examples: **1** $\sqrt{\frac{9}{16}} = \frac{\sqrt{9}}{\sqrt{16}} = \frac{3}{4}$

2 $\sqrt{6\frac{1}{4}} = \sqrt{\frac{25}{4}} = \frac{5}{2} = 2\frac{1}{2}$

Calculate the following without using your calculator.

1 $\sqrt{\frac{1}{9}} =$ ____________

2 $\sqrt{\frac{25}{36}} =$ ____________

3 $\sqrt{3\frac{1}{16}} =$ ____________

4 $\sqrt{2\frac{2}{49}} =$ ____________

5 $\sqrt[3]{\frac{8}{27}} =$ ____________

6 $\sqrt[4]{\frac{16}{81}} =$ ____________

 ISBN: 9780170447010

Ordering and comparing fractions

Ordering fractions

Ordering fractions is easiest if they all have the same denominator.

Example: Which is larger, $\frac{3}{\mathbf{4}}$ or $\frac{5}{\mathbf{7}}$?

The **LCM** of **4** and **7** is 28, so use **28** as a denominator:

$\frac{3}{4} = \frac{\mathbf{21}}{\mathbf{28}}$ and $\frac{5}{7} = \frac{\mathbf{20}}{\mathbf{28}}$. So, $\frac{3}{4} > \frac{5}{7}$.

In the second row, rewrite the fractions in the first row so they have the same denominator.
In the third row, write the fractions in the top row in ascending order.

1

$\frac{5}{6}$	$\frac{7}{12}$	$\frac{3}{4}$	$\frac{1}{2}$	$\frac{5}{8}$	$\frac{2}{3}$	$\frac{5}{12}$	$\frac{7}{8}$
					$\frac{16}{24}$		

Smallest ... Largest

				$\frac{2}{3}$			

2

$\frac{7}{10}$	$\frac{5}{6}$	$\frac{2}{3}$	$\frac{4}{5}$	$\frac{3}{4}$	$\frac{7}{12}$	$\frac{13}{20}$	$\frac{8}{15}$

Smallest ... Largest

3

$\frac{1}{4}$	$\frac{2}{7}$	$\frac{5}{14}$	$\frac{3}{7}$	$\frac{11}{28}$	$\frac{3}{14}$	$\frac{3}{8}$	$\frac{1}{2}$

Smallest ... Largest

ISBN: 9780170447010

Comparing fractions

Symbols you need to know:

- > means '**is greater than**'
- < means '**is less than**'
- ≥ means '**is greater than or equal to**'
- ≤ means '**is less than or equal to**'

Insert any of the four symbols above, in order to create true statements.

1 $8 \ \square \ 7$

2 $-1 \ \square \ 1$

3 $-10 \ \square \ -11$

4 $10^0 \ \square \ 10$

5 $10^6 \ \square \ 999\,999$

6 $30 \ \square \ 2^5$

To compare fractions

- As with ordering fractions, rewrite the fractions so they have the same denominator.

Example: Which fraction is greater, $\frac{8}{\mathbf{11}}$ or $\frac{5}{\mathbf{7}}$?

Denominators are **11** and **7**, so the common denominator is **77**.

So $\frac{8}{11} \times \frac{7}{7} = \frac{56}{\mathbf{77}}$ and $\frac{5}{7} \times \frac{11}{11} = \frac{55}{\mathbf{77}}$ $\therefore$ $\frac{56}{77} > \frac{55}{77}$, so $\frac{8}{11} > \frac{5}{7}$.

Rewrite each of the following pairs of fractions so that they have a common denominator, and then insert a < or > sign in the box between them.

7 $\frac{2}{3} \ \square \ \frac{5}{7}$

$= \frac{14}{21}$ $\qquad = \frac{\square}{\square}$

8 $\frac{3}{4} \ \square \ \frac{7}{9}$

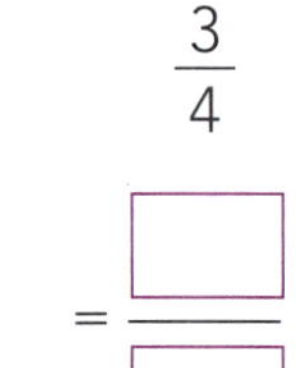

$= \frac{\square}{\square}$ $\qquad = \frac{\square}{\square}$

9 $\frac{7}{8} \ \square \ \frac{6}{7}$

$= \frac{\square}{\square}$ $\qquad = \frac{\square}{\square}$

10 $\frac{2}{7} \ \square \ \frac{3}{11}$

$= \frac{\square}{\square}$ $\qquad = \frac{\square}{\square}$

11 $\frac{7}{12} \ \square \ \frac{4}{7}$

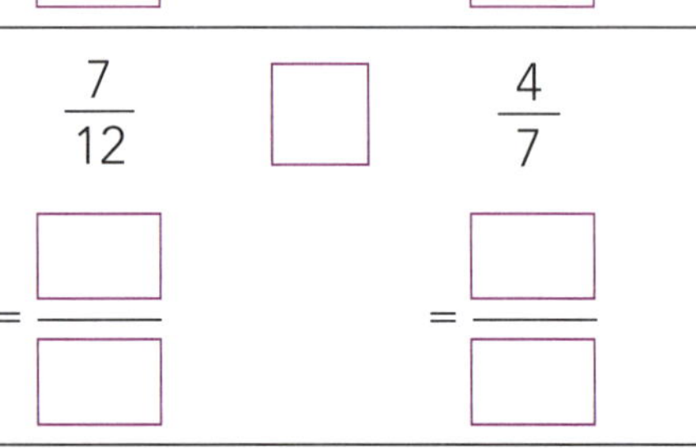

$= \frac{\square}{\square}$ $\qquad = \frac{\square}{\square}$

12 $\frac{13}{20} \ \square \ \frac{2}{3}$

$= \frac{\square}{\square}$ $\qquad = \frac{\square}{\square}$

ISBN: 9780170447010

Fractions of a quantity

Remember that '**of**' means you must '**multiply**'.

Example:

$$\frac{2}{3} \textbf{ of } 50 = \frac{2}{3} \times 50$$
$$= \frac{2}{3} \times \frac{50}{1}$$
$$= \frac{100}{3}$$
$$= 33\frac{1}{3}$$

Replace the word '**of**' with a **x** sign.

Remember that '50' means 50 wholes, or $\frac{50}{1}$.

Answer the following questions.

1 $\frac{1}{7}$ of 56 = ______________________

= ______________________

2 $\frac{4}{5}$ of 45 = ______________________

= ______________________

3 $\frac{3}{8}$ of 28 = ______________________

= ______________________

4 $\frac{5}{6}$ of 25 = ______________________

= ______________________

5 $\frac{2}{9}$ of 330 = ______________________

= ______________________

6 $\frac{3}{2}$ of 17 = ______________________

= ______________________

7 $1\frac{3}{4}$ of 12 = ______________________

= ______________________

= ______________________

8 For the school production, $\frac{5}{12}$ of the tickets were sold to students. A total of 492 tickets were sold. How many tickets were sold to people other than students?

____

9 A flat which houses six students has two single and two double rooms. Those that share a double room pay $\frac{3}{15}$ of the total rent between them, and the two in single rooms pay the rest.

- Calculate the fraction of the rent paid by each person.
- If the rent is \$540 per week, calculate how much each person pays.

____

____

ISBN: 9780170447010

Mixing it up

Answer the following questions, and show your reasoning.

1 a There is $\frac{2}{3}$ of a pizza left. If this is shared equally between five children, what fraction of the whole pizza would each child get?

____

b However, Mel got up first, and she ate $\frac{1}{4}$ of the remaining two thirds of the pizza. What fraction of the whole pizza did Mel eat?

____

c What fraction of the whole pizza will be left for the other four children?

____

d If this is shared equally between the other four children, what fraction of the whole pizza does each child get?

____

e Adam is one of the children. How much more pizza did Mel get than Adam?

____

2 Tara grows courgettes and scallopini and sells the plants in the market. The seeds come in mixed packets, and both scallopini and courgettes can be green or yellow.

- She finds that $\frac{10}{11}$ of her seeds germinate.
- Of those that germinate, $\frac{3}{5}$ produce courgettes, and the rest are scallopini.
- $\frac{4}{9}$ of the courgettes are yellow.
- $\frac{5}{12}$ of the scallopini are green.
- She planted 66 seeds in total.

Calculate:
- the fraction of all the seeds that produced each type of scallopini and courgette plant, and
- the numbers of each type that she will have available for sale.

____

____

____

ISBN: 9780170447010

Decimals

Place value

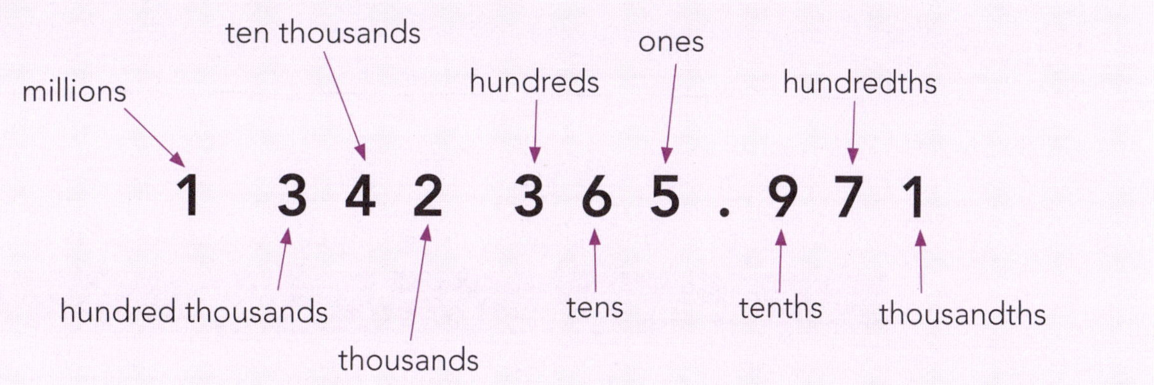

When converting numerals to words, split the number where the **gaps** occur.

Examples: 1 Write 12 384 562 in words.

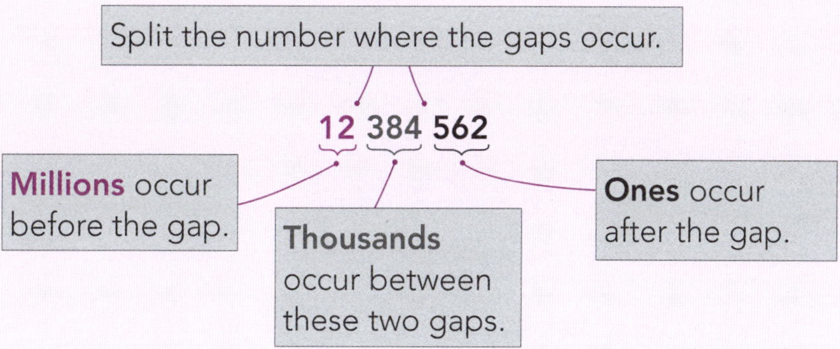

Twelve million, **three hundred and eighty-four thousand**, **five hundred and sixty-two** (ones).

2 Write 193 125 764.38 in words.

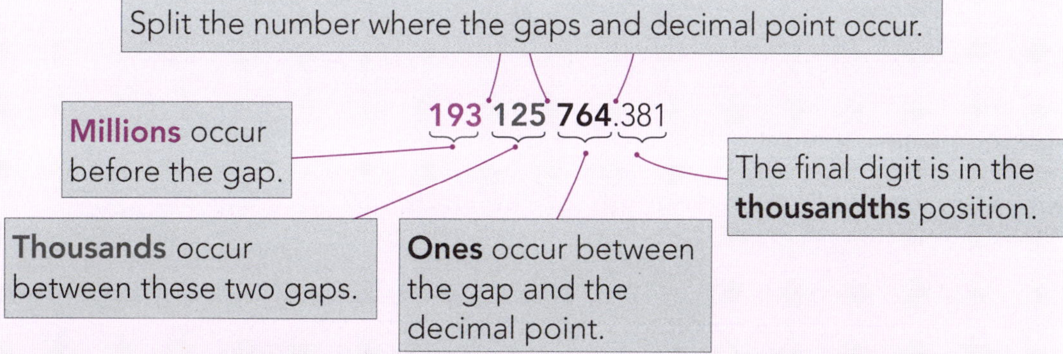

One hundred and ninety-three million, **one hundred and twenty-five thousand**, **seven hundred and sixty-four** and three hundred and eighty-one thousandths.

Write down the value of the purple numerals as numbers and in words.

		Number	Words
1	259 176	50 000	
2	318 627 054		Ten million
3	721 469 123		
4	123 456 980		

Write down the value of the purple numerals as decimals, fractions and in words.

		Decimal	Fraction	Words
5	0.192		———	One tenth or one hundred thousandths
6	0.163		$\frac{3}{1\,000}$	
7	24.057	0.05	———	

Write numbers using words.

8 41 762 391

____

9 30 017

____

10 108 045 006

____

11 40 002 013

____

Write numbers using numerals.

12 Twelve million, two thousand and ninety-three ______________

13 Seventy and eighteen thousandths ______________

14 Thirteen thousand and twenty-seven and four thousandths ______________

15 Twelve million, three hundred and six thousand and five hundredths ______________

ISBN: 9780170447010

Decimals on number lines

Here is how to work out the size of each gap between ticks on a number line.

Step 1: Calculate the **distance** between two **labelled** points.
Distance = 0.750 – 0.715 = **0.035**.

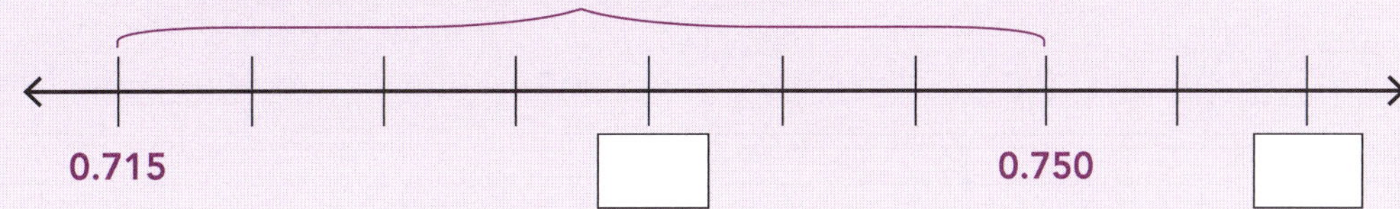

Step 2: Count the **number of gaps** between 0.715 and 0.750. **Number of gaps** = 7.

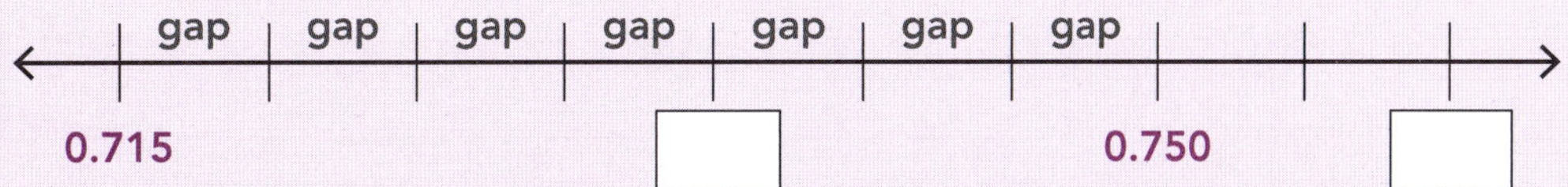

Step 3: Divide the distance by the number of gaps: $\frac{0.035}{7}$ = 0.005.

Step 4: Add 0.005 after each gap along the number line.

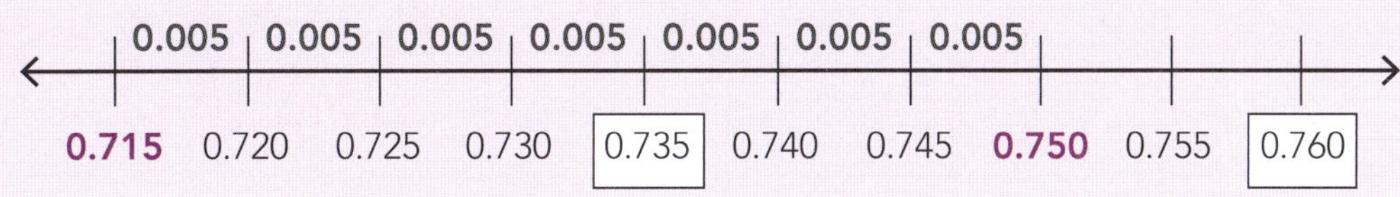

Calculate the size of each gap and write the missing decimals on the number lines.

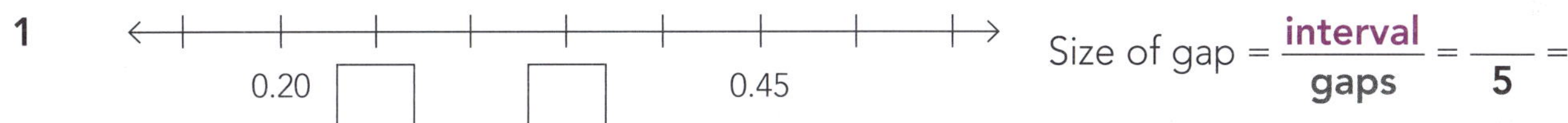

1 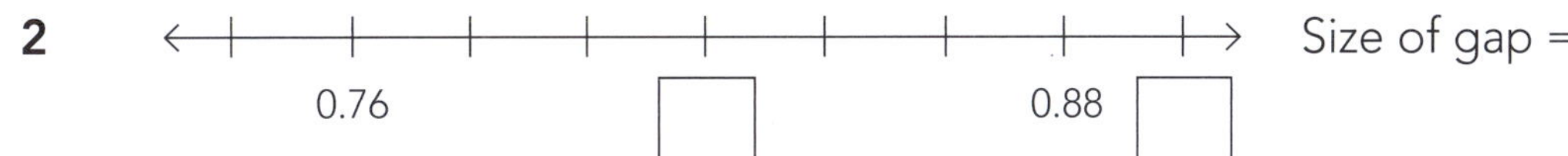

Size of gap = $\frac{\text{interval}}{\text{gaps}} = \frac{\quad}{5} =$

2 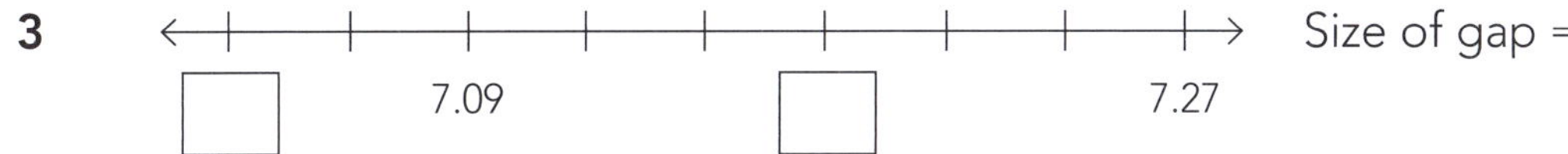

Size of gap =

3 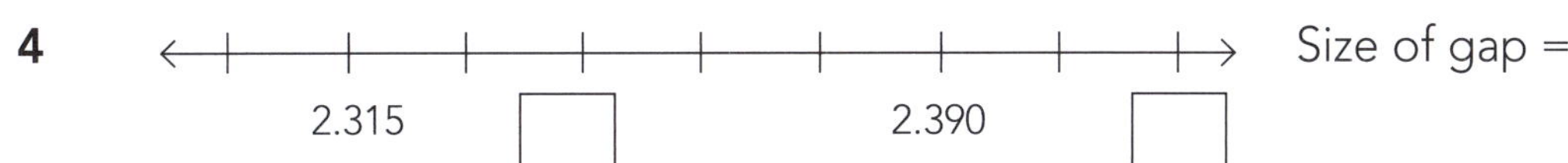

Size of gap =

4 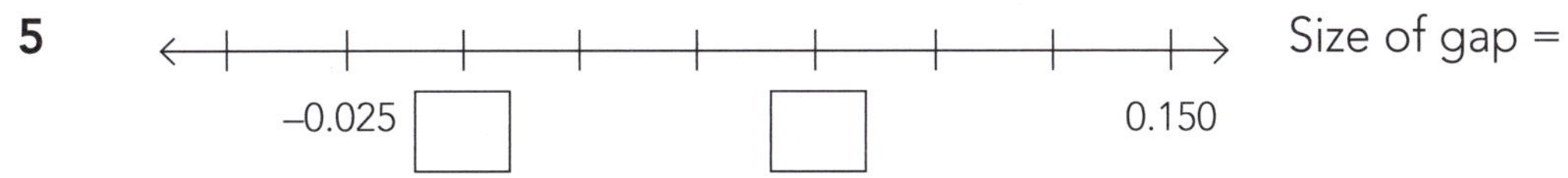

Size of gap =

5

Size of gap =

ISBN: 9780170447010

6 Write decimal values for each point along the number line. Choose the most appropriate values from the list below. You will not need all the points on the list.

0.079	0.031	0.012	0.053	−0.025	0.01
0	−0.015	0.048	0.102	0.018	0.015
0.006	0.02	0.084	−0.008	0.074	0.023

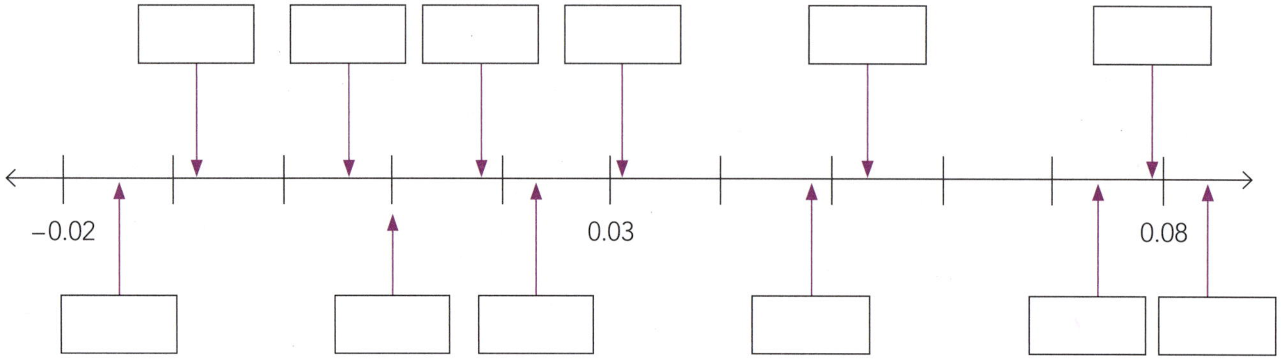

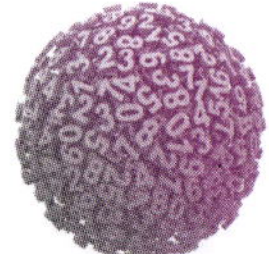

Challenge 2

1 Write decimal values for each point along the number line. Choose the most appropriate values from the list below. You will not need all the points on the list.

−0.019	0.025	−0.032	−0.003	0.005	−0.013
0.001	0.0025	0.003	−0.023	−0.030	0.030
−0.026	−0.039	0.005	−0.040	−0.008	−0.0425

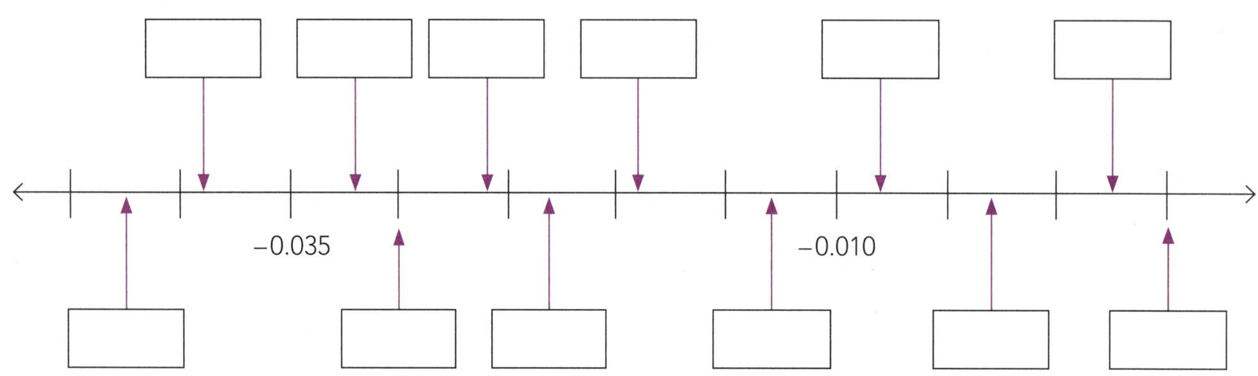

ISBN: 9780170447010

Comparing decimals

- To determine which decimal is larger or smaller, you need to consider the place values of each digit, starting from the left.

Example: Place a **<** or a **>** sign between the pair of decimals.

10.0110 □ 10.0101

Remember, **<** and **>** symbols **point to the smaller** number.

Step 1: Arrange the numbers with the **decimal points lined up** vertically:

10.0110
10.0101

The decimal points **must** be in line.

Step 2: Start at the left, and look for the **first pair of digits that is different**:

The first **four** digits are the same.

10.01 | **10**
10.01 | **01**

Step 3: Decide which is larger or smaller: **1** > **0**, so 10.0110 **>** 10.0101.

Place a > or < or = to make each statement true.

1 53.101 □ 53.110

2 0.2797 □ 0.2779

3 1.2300 □ 1.230

4 454.099 □ 454.100

5 19.1919 □ 19.1920

6 8.51499 □ 8.5149

Write down the following decimals.

7 0.219 increased by two thousandths __________

8 14.008 increased by three thousandths __________

9 26.095 increased by seven hundredths __________

10 10.030 increased by five tenths __________

11 9.4631 decreased by thirty-seven thousandths __________

Place these decimals in ascending order (smallest to largest).

12 5.0500 5.5050 5.0505 5.0055 ______ ______ ______ ______

13 0.1110 0.1101 0.1010 0.1011 ______ ______ ______ ______

ISBN: 9780170447010

Recurring decimals

- Recurring decimals are decimals that have a pattern of repeating digits which never stops.
- To identify these, a dot is placed over the first and last digits that repeat.

Examples: **1** 0.3333333… can be written as $0.\dot{3}$.

2 1.2373737… can be written as $1.2\dot{3}\dot{7}$. — Notice that only the digits with dots are repeated.

3 0.40740740… can be written as $0.\dot{4}0\dot{7}$. — This means that the 407 must be repeated.

Why are these important?

Compare: 0.6 of \$1 000 = \$600

$0.\dot{6}$ of \$1 000 = \$666.67 — That's a difference of nearly \$67!

More examples:

Fraction	Decimal	Notation
$\frac{2}{9}$	0.222222…	$0.\dot{2}$
$\frac{4}{11}$	0.363636…	$0.\dot{3}\dot{6}$
$\frac{2}{15}$	0.1333333…	$0.1\dot{3}$

Fraction	Decimal	Notation
$\frac{7}{22}$	0.3181818…	$0.3\dot{1}\dot{8}$
$\frac{10}{27}$	0.3703703…	$0.\dot{3}7\dot{0}$
$\frac{2}{7}$	0.285714285714…	$0.\dot{2}8571\dot{4}$

Write these decimals in full. Use '…' at the end to show that they carry on.

1 $0.\dot{2}$ = ______________________ **2** $0.\dot{8}\dot{1}$ = ______________________

3 $0.\dot{6}0\dot{5}$ = ______________________ **4** $0.3\dot{4}98\dot{7}$ = ______________________

Write these using recurring decimal notation.

5 0.494949… = ______________________ **6** 0.349349349… = ______________________

7 0.000666666… = ______________________ **8** 0.81512512512… = ______________________

Write these fractions using recurring decimal notation.

9 $\frac{4}{9}$ = ______________________ **10** $\frac{5}{11}$ = ______________________

11 $6\frac{8}{15}$ = ______________________ **12** $10\frac{8}{27}$ = ______________________

ISBN: 9780170447010

Turning decimals into fractions

Steps:

1 Write the decimal as a fraction with a denominator of 10^n, where n = the number of decimal places.

2 Cancel if you can.

Examples:

1 $0.54 = \frac{54}{100} = \frac{27}{50}$ (÷ 2)

0.54 has 2 decimal places, so $0.54 = \frac{54}{10^2}$

2

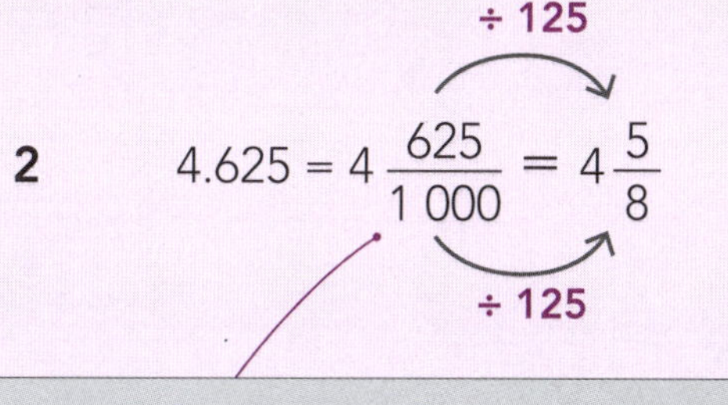

$4.625 = 4\frac{625}{1\,000} = 4\frac{5}{8}$ (÷ 125)

0.625 has 3 decimal places, so $4.625 = 4\frac{625}{10^3}$

- You can also use your calculator to convert between the two by using the

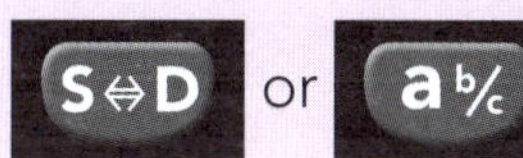

or
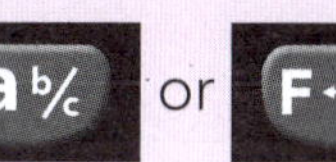

or

button.

Without using your calculator, convert the following decimals into fractions.

1 0.22 = ____________________
= ____________________

2 0.125 = ____________________
= ____________________

3 2.14 = ____________________
= ____________________

4 10.55 = ____________________
= ____________________

5 7.64 = ____________________
= ____________________

6 0.155 = ____________________
= ____________________

7 6.136 = ____________________
= ____________________

8 0.1096 = ____________________
= ____________________

ISBN: 9780170447010

Turning recurring decimals into fractions

(using a little bit of algebra)

Steps:

1 Call the recurring decimal x.
2 Let n be the number of recurring digits.
3 Multiply the recurring decimal by 10^n.
4 Subtract x from the result in step 3.
5 Solve to find x, simplifying if necessary.

Examples:

1

$$x = 0.\dot{8} = 0.8888\ldots$$

$$10x = 8.8888\ldots$$

$$10x - x = 8.8888\ldots - 0.8888\ldots$$

$$9x = 8$$

$$x = \frac{8}{9}$$

$0.\dot{8}$ has one recurring digit, so multiply by 10^1.

Subtracting x from $10x$ gets rid of the recurring decimal.

2

$$x = 0.\dot{1}2\dot{3} = 0.123123\ldots$$

$$1\,000x = 123.123123\ldots$$

$$1\,000x - x = 123.123123\ldots - 0.123123\ldots$$

$$999x = 123$$

$$x = \frac{123}{999} = \frac{41}{333} \quad (\div 3 \text{ top and bottom})$$

$0.\dot{1}2\dot{3}$ has three recurring digits, so multiply by 10^3.

Subtracting x from $1\,000x$ gets rid of the recurring decimal.

Note: This method needs to be modified for decimals in which some digits do not recur, such as $0.3\dot{6}$, $2.3\dot{1}\dot{8}$, $0.0\dot{1}2\dot{3}$, etc.

Use this method to convert the following recurring decimals into fractions.

1 $0.\dot{2}$

____

____

____

____

2 $0.\dot{1}\dot{5}$

____

____

____

____

 ISBN: 9780170447010

3 $0.\dot{9}\dot{0}$

4 $0.\dot{5}1\dot{8}$

5 $0.\dot{9}6\dot{2}$

6 $0.\dot{1}3\dot{5}$

7 **a** Use the method to show that $0.\dot{1}4285\dot{7} = \frac{1}{7}$.

b **Weird stuff:** Use your calculator to help you to complete the next two rows of the table.

Fraction	Decimal
$\frac{1}{7}$	$0.\dot{1}4285\dot{7}$
$\frac{2}{7}$	
$\frac{3}{7}$	

c Use your answers in **b** to help you predict the decimals needed to complete the table. Use your calculator to check your answers.

Fraction	Decimal
$\frac{4}{7}$	
$\frac{5}{7}$	
$\frac{6}{7}$	

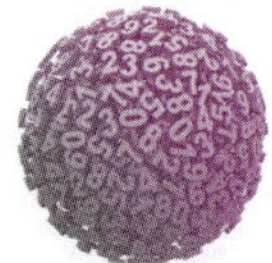

Challenge 3

Numbers in base 2

Here is one way of viewing our number system:

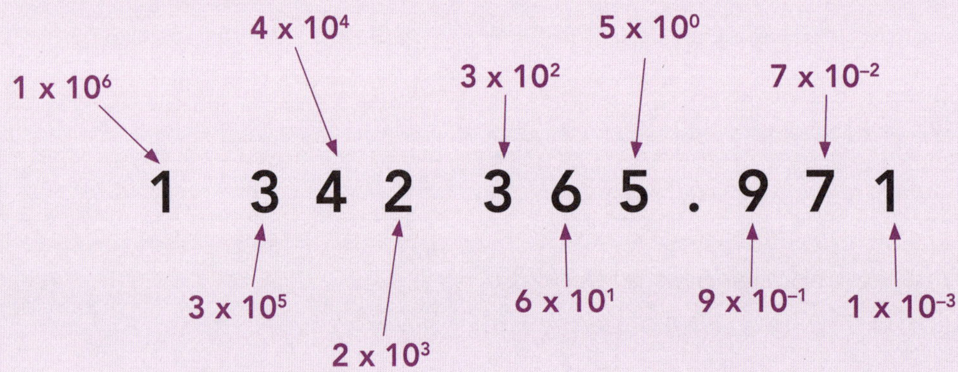

- In order to name the numbers between 10^0 and 10^1, we need the **10** numerals: 0, 1, 2, 3, 4, 5, 6, 7, 8 and 9.
- As a result, we say our number system is organised on a **base of 10**.

Thousands	Hundreds	Tens	Ones	·	Tenths	Hundredths
1 000	100	10	1	·	$\frac{1}{10^1} = \frac{1}{10}$ or 0.1	$\frac{1}{10^2} = \frac{1}{100}$ or 0.01
10^3	10^2	10^1	10^0	·	10^{-1}	10^{-2}

A number system with a base of 2

- A **base 2** number system needs just **two** numerals: **0** and **1**.
- This is also known as a **binary** system.
- Computers are coded in binary because electrical signals can be only **on** or **off**.

Eights	Fours	Twos	Ones	·	Halves	Quarters
8	4	2	1	·	$\frac{1}{2^1} = \frac{1}{2}$ or 0.5	$\frac{1}{2^2} = \frac{1}{4}$ or 0.05
2^3	2^2	2^1	2^0	·	2^{-1}	2^{-2}

ISBN: 9780170447010

Converting base 2 numbers into base 10 numbers

Examples:

Number in base 2	$2^4 = 16$	$2^3 = 8$	$2^2 = 4$	$2^1 = 2$	$2^0 = 1$		$2^{-1} = \frac{1}{2}$	Number in base 10
10				1	0			**2**
101			1	0	1			**5**
1011		1	0	1	1			**11**
11010	1	1	0	1	0			**26**
11.1				1	1	•	1	$3\frac{1}{2}$
11111.1	1	1	1	1	1	•	1	$31\frac{1}{2}$

1 Use the table to help you convert the following base 2 numbers into base 10 numbers.

Number in base 2	$2^5 = 32$	$2^4 = 16$	$2^3 = 8$	$2^2 = 4$	$2^1 = 2$	$2^0 = 1$	Number in base 10
11					1	1	
110				1	1	0	
1000			1	0	0	0	
10111		1	0	1	1	1	
100100	1	0	0	1	0	0	
111011	1	1	1	0	1	1	

Convert the following base 2 numbers into base 10 numbers.

2 111 = ____________________

3 1110 = ____________________

4 10011 = ____________________

5 1000000 = ____________________

6 11001 = ____________________

7 110001 = ____________________

8 1001.1 = ____________________

9 100.01 = ____________________

10 1101.11 = ____________________

11 0.111 = ____________________

ISBN: 9780170447010

Converting base 10 numbers into base 2 numbers

Repeatedly divide the number by 2, and record the remainders.

Examples:

1 Convert 23 into a base 2 number.

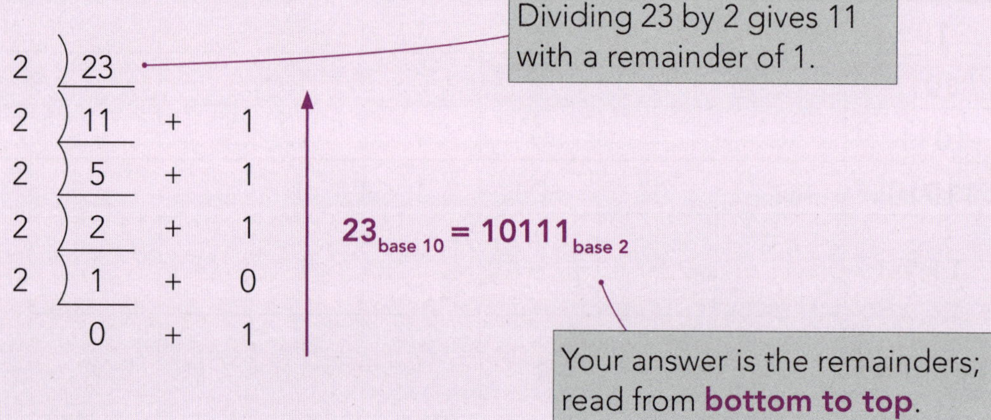

Check: 10111 = 1 x 16 + **0** x 8 + **1** x 4 + **1** x 2 + **1** x 1 = **23**

2 Convert 96 to a base 2 number.

2) 96
2) 48 + 0
2) 24 + 0
2) 12 + 0
2) 6 + 0
2) 3 + 0
2) 1 + 1
0 + 1

$96_{\text{base 10}} = 1100000_{\text{base 2}}$

Check: 1100000 = 1 x 64 + **1** x 32 + **0** x 16 + **0** x 8 + **0** x 4 + **0** x 2 + **0** x 1 = **96**

Convert the following base 10 numbers into base 2 numbers.

12 12 = ____________________ **13** 17 = ____________________

ISBN: 9780170447010

14 29 = ____________

15 35 = ____________

16 60.5 = ____________

17 100.75 = ____________

18 In the table below, write the first five Mersenne prime numbers, and then convert each into a base 2 number. Reminder: Mersenne primes take the form $2^n - 1$.

Mersenne prime	Base 10	Base 2
$2^2 - 1$		
	7	
$2^{11} - 1$		

19 What do you notice about these Mersenne primes when they are written in base 2?

____

____

20 Give an explanation for your answer to question **19**.

____

____

____

____

ISBN: 9780170447010

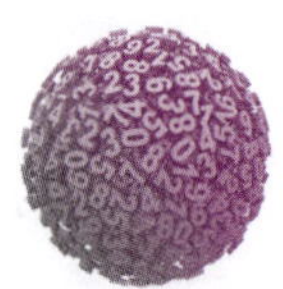

Percentages

- Percentages are a way of expressing a number **out of 100**.

Example:

38 out of 100 squares are purple.

$\frac{38}{100}$ is the same as 38%.

62 out of 100 squares are white.

$\frac{62}{100}$ is the same as 62%.

38 purple squares.

100 squares altogether.

100 – 38 = 62 white squares.

Converting between decimals and percentages

Because percentages are out of 100,

- to change a decimal to a percentage, you **multiply by 100**
- to change a percentage to a decimal, you **divide by 100**.

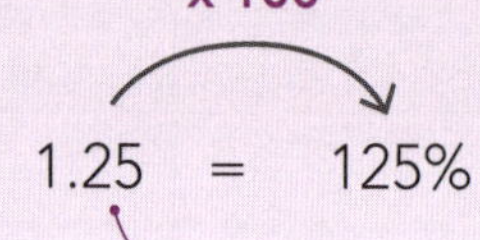

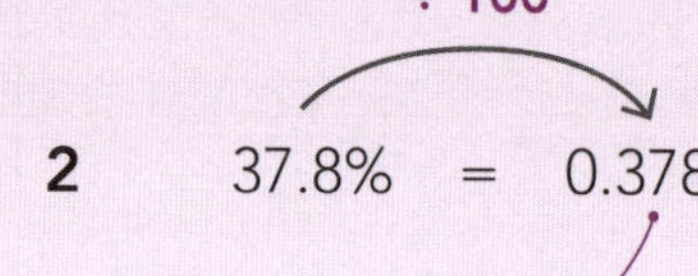

Examples: **1** 1.25 = 125% **2** 37.8% = 0.378

Notice that **multiplying** by 100 is the same as moving the decimal point two places to the **right**.

Notice that **dividing** by 100 is the same as moving the decimal point two places to the **left**.

Convert the following decimals into percentages.

1 0.21 = ____________________ **2** 0.0649 = ____________________

3 0.0075 = ____________________ **4** 3.04 = ____________________

Convert the following percentages into decimals.

5 71% = ____________________ **6** 4.8% = ____________________

7 0.6% = ____________________ **8** 273% = ____________________

 ISBN: 9780170447010

Converting between fractions and percentages

Fractions to percentages: If possible, use equivalent fractions to make the denominator 100.

Examples: **1** $\frac{6}{25} = \frac{24}{100} = 24\%$ (× 4 numerator and denominator)

2 $\frac{82}{200} = \frac{41}{100} = 41\%$ (÷ 2 numerator and denominator)

Remember, you must multiply or divide both numerator and denominator by the **same number**.

- If this is too hard, use your calculator to multiply the fraction by 100, or use the % button on your calculator.

Percentages to fractions: Use equivalent fractions to simplify the fraction.

1 $48\% = \frac{48}{100} = \frac{12}{25}$

2 $12.5\% = \frac{12.5}{100} = \frac{25}{200} = \frac{1}{8}$

Avoid having combinations of fractions and decimals.

Fill in the gaps.

	Fraction	Decimal	Percentage
1			15%
2	$\frac{7}{25}$		
3	$\frac{3}{8}$		
4		0.246	
5		1.75	
6			62.5%
7	$2\frac{3}{5}$		
8		0.005	

ISBN: 9780170447010

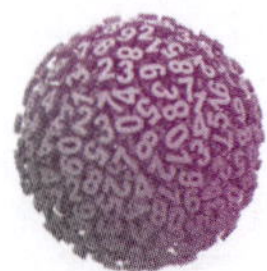

Challenge 4

Place the numbers in the list below in ascending order.
Hint: Change them all to decimals first.

1

$\frac{2}{7}$	27.5%	$0.28\dot{3}$	$\frac{4}{15}$	29%	$\frac{5}{17}$	0.285	$\frac{5}{18}$
0.2857			$0.2\dot{6}$				

Smallest | Largest

$\frac{4}{15}$							

2

$0.708\dot{3}$	$\frac{22}{31}$	$0.\dot{7}\dot{2}$	$\frac{19}{27}$	0.71	72.5%	$\frac{18}{25}$	70.5%

Smallest | Largest

3

$0.04\dot{5}$	4.5%	$\frac{2}{37}$	0.05	$\frac{1}{21}$	$\frac{3}{65}$	$0.0\dot{5}$	5.4%

Smallest | Largest

4

$1.\dot{1}\dot{5}$	$1\frac{3}{20}$	$1.\dot{1}6\dot{2}$	114.9%	$\frac{7}{6}$	1.1515	$1\frac{4}{27}$	115.6%

Smallest | Largest

ISBN: 9780170447010

Calculating percentages

- Remember, 'percent' means out of 100, so turning a fraction into a percentage means **multiplying by 100**.

Example: The area of Antarctica is 14 200 000 km^2. Of this, 13 916 000 km^2 is ice and the rest is rock. What percentage of Antarctica is ice?

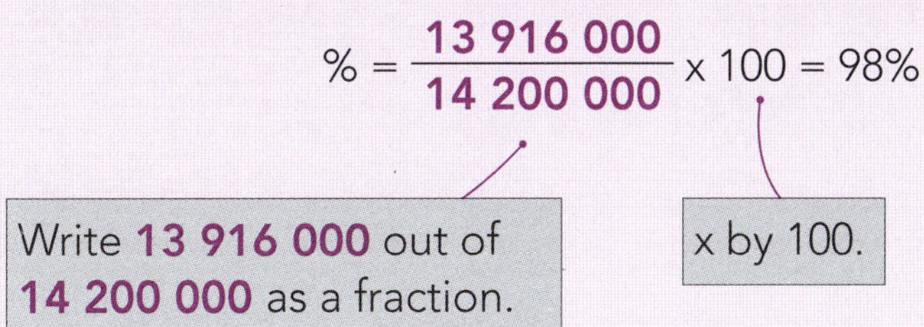

Write the following amounts as percentages.

1 45 out of 180 = ____________________

= ____________________

2 96 out of 120 = ____________________

= ____________________

3 1.5 out of 60 = ____________________

= ____________________

4 145 out of 10 000 = ____________________

= ____________________

5 104.4 out of 290 = ____________________

= ____________________

6 875 out of 7 000 = ____________________

= ____________________

7 A cucumber weighing 400 g contains 384 g water. What percentage of a cucumber is water?

____

8 An NBA basketball lasts for 10 000 bounces. The number of bounces in an average NBA game is 2 650. What percentage of the life of an NBA ball is used up during a single NBA basketball game?

____

9 In a book written in English, an average page contains 500 words, and each word is on average 4.8 letters long. If there are 300 of the letter 'e' on an average page, what percentage of letters in the English text are the letter 'e'?

____

10 In 2018, 21 people died in the USA as a result of being struck by lightning. Of these, 17 were males. What percentage of those killed by lightning were men?

____

ISBN: 9780170447010

Finding percentages of amounts

- There are many ways of doing this.

Examples:

1 Find 2% of 350.

You should be able to do this without a calculator.

Either: convert the percentage to a decimal: 2% **of** 350 = 0.02 **x** 350
= 7

Remember, '**of**' means **x**.

Or: convert the percentage to a fraction: 2% **of** 350 = $\frac{2}{100}$ **x** 350
= 7

Or: for some numbers, find 10% and then multiply or divide:

10% **of** 350 = 35

2% of 350 = $\frac{35}{5}$ = 7

- Sometimes the numbers are not easy, so use your **calculator**.
- Not all calculators are the same, so you will need to experiment until you find how yours works. Two possibilities are shown in the box below.

2 Find 85% of $3 400.

85% of $3 400 = $2 890

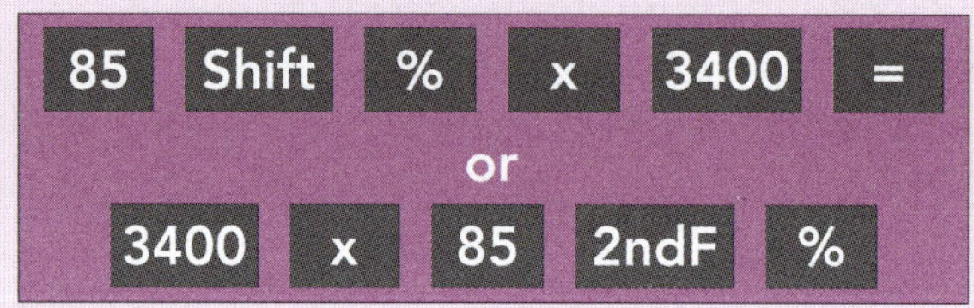

Calculate these without using a calculator.

1 15% of 60 = ______________
= ______________

2 25% of 72 = ______________
= ______________

3 0.5% of 700 = ______________
= ______________

4 110% of 240 = ______________
= ______________

Use your calculator to work out these answers.

5 36% of 72 = ______________

6 105% of 660 = ______________

7 7.5% of 3 600 = ______________

8 0.7% of 500 000 = ______________

9 Eight percent of people have an extra rib. If your school has 825 students, how many would be expected to have an extra rib?

____

 ISBN: 9780170447010

10 Koalas sleep for at least 75% of the day because gum leaves take such a long time to be digested. What is the minimum number of hours that a koala spends sleeping during each day?

11 The trunk of Tane Mahuta, a giant kauri tree in Northland, has an estimated mass of 13 666 800 kg. Plants can contain 0.000001% of gold. Use these numbers to estimate how much gold is in the trunk of Tane Mahuta.

Mixing it up

1 Ninety percent of the earth's population lives in the northern hemisphere. If the population of the earth is 7.53 billion, how many people live in the southern hemisphere? Write your answer in numerals.

2 **a** An average-sized female vampire bat weighs 30 g, and she gives birth to young which weigh on average 8 g. (She does this while hanging upside down, and she has to catch the baby!) Calculate the weight of the baby bat as a percentage of the mother's weight.

b An average-sized human female weighs 70 kg. What would a human baby weigh if it was the same percentage of the mother's weight?

3 The leg bones of bats are so thin that only two species out of the 1 200 species can walk on the ground. What percentage of the species of bat can walk on the ground?

4 A cow produces (farts) 120 kg of methane a year. The table shows the amount of methane produced each year by a human, a pig and a sheep. Complete the table.

	kg methane produced per year	as a % of the methane produced by a cow
Human		0.1%
Pig	1.5	
Sheep		$6.\dot{6}\%$

ISBN: 9780170447010

Increasing by an amount

- There are several ways of doing this.

Example:

Increase 92 by 25%. — This means that we need 100% plus 25%.

Increased amount = 92 + 25% of 92
= 92 + 23
= 115

or

Increased amount = 92 x 125%
= 92 x 1.25
= 115

Calculate these.

1 Increase 60 by 15%.

2 Increase 24 by 75%.

3 Increase $450 by 40%.

4 Increase 480 g by 12.5%.

5 Increase 68 kg by 35%.

6 Increase 75 km by 15%.

7 Increase $1 600 by 12%.

8 Increase 7.6 t by 8%.

9 A small town has a population of 1 200. If it grows by 6%, what will be the new population?

10 Tamati is paid $18 per hour for gardening. If he is given a 5% increase, what will be his new pay rate?

11 When soft drink freezes, its volume increases by 9%. If you put a 600 mL bottle of soft drink in the freezer to cool it down, but you forget to take it out, what is volume of the frozen soft drink?

12 The average volume of milk produced by a cow during each milking when no music is played is 8.7 L. Playing slow music to cows during milking increases their yield by 3%. Calculate the average volume produced if slow music is played.

ISBN: 9780170447010

Decreasing by an amount

- Once again, there are several ways of doing this.

Example:

Decrease 140 by 15%.

This means that we need 100% minus 15%.

Decreased amount = 140 – 15% of 140
= 140 – 21
= 119

or

Decreased amount = 140 x 85%
= 140 x 0.85
= 119

Calculate these.

1 Decrease 96 by 25%.

2 Decrease 124 by 20%.

3 Decrease $640 by 15%.

4 Decrease 480 g by 37.5%.

5 Decrease 90 kg by 5%.

6 Decrease 96 km by 12%.

7 Decrease $875 by 3%.

8 Decrease 28 t by 16%.

9 The value of a $345 000 house decreases by 2%. What is its decreased value?

10 A sale advertisement says '15% off everything'. Calculate the sale price of:

a a pair of jeans that are normally $125.00.

b a hoodie that is normally $98.00.

11 A rat control programme was introduced to a large area of bush, and 1 200 rats were trapped and killed in its first year. If the number of rats caught decreased by 16% in the second year, how many were caught during the second year?

ISBN: 9780170447010

Finding a percentage increase or decrease

Examples:

1 The value of a painting increased from \$650 to \$728. Calculate the percentage increase in its value.

Step 1: **Subtract** the amounts: $\$728 - \$650 = \$78$

Step 2: **Divide** the difference by the **original** quantity, then multiply by 100. $\frac{78}{650} \times 100 = 12\%$

2 The original price of a dress was \$82, and its sale price is \$61.50. Calculate the percentage reduction in its price.

Step 1: **Subtract** the amounts: $\$82 - \$61.50 = \$20.50$

Step 2: **Divide** the difference by the **original** quantity, then multiply by 100. $\frac{20.5}{82} \times 100 = 25\%$

Calculate the percentage changes below.

1 From 90 to 108.

2 From 240 to 156.

3 From 24 g to 27.6 g.

4 From \$168 to \$147.

5 From \$960 to \$998.40.

6 From 0.56 g to 0.532 g.

7 From \$624 000 to \$661 440.

8 From \$1 280.00 to \$1 305.60.

9 A \$48 shirt has a sale price of \$42. Calculate the percentage reduction.

10 Tania's rent went from \$240 per week last year to \$246 this year. Calculate the percentage increase.

ISBN: 9780170447010

Mixing it up

1 GST (Goods and Services Tax) of 15% is added to the cost of all items that you buy and services that you pay for. Calculate the retail price of a phone if the pre-GST price is $550.

____

2 You can calculate the pre-GST price of an item by dividing by 1.15. A computer monitor retails for $184. Calculate its pre-GST price.

____

3 A shop advertisements states: 'We pay the GST. You save 15%!'. Investigate this statement. Hint: Consider an item that costs $100 excluding GST.

____

____

Complete the tables to find some surprising answers.

4 Mel has a jar containing 200 marbles, 99% of which are blue and the rest are red. How many blue marbles must be removed from the jar in order to make the percentage of blue marbles 98%, and how many marbles will be left in the jar?

Start:

Blue	Red
99%	_____ %
_____ marbles	2 marbles

Finish:

Blue	Red
98%	_____ %
_____ marbles	_____ marbles

∴ She needs to remove ____ blue marbles, so there will be ____ marbles in the jar.

5 Alice is dehydrating plums. Plum flesh is 85% water, and the instructions say that the water content should be 25% when the process is completed. If she started with 10 kg of plums, what will the dehydrated plums weigh? Note: During dehydration, only water is removed.

Start:

Water	Plum
85%	_____ %
_____ kg	_____ kg

Finish:

Water	Plum
25%	_____ %
_____ kg	_____ kg

∴ The dehydrated weight will be ____ kg.

ISBN: 9780170447010

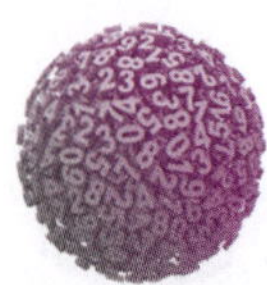

Groups of numbers

Real numbers (R)

Rational numbers (Q)
Can be expressed as a fraction.
Includes terminating and recurring decimals.
e.g. $\frac{3}{7}$, 1.49, $0.8\dot{1}\dot{3}$

Integers (*I*)
..., −4, −3, −2, −1

Whole numbers (*W*)
0

Natural or counting numbers (*N*)
1, 2, 3, 4, ...

Irrational numbers (Q′)
Non-terminating decimals including surds.
e.g. $\sqrt{2}$, π

ISBN: 9780170447010

1 The **natural (or counting) numbers** form the smallest group of numbers.

Write out the first 10 natural numbers:

____

2 The **whole numbers** include the natural numbers and ______________.

Write out the first 10 whole numbers:

____

3 The **integers** include the whole numbers plus negative values of the natural numbers.

Write out 11 integers, starting at –5:

____

4 The **rational numbers** include the integers and all numbers that can be written as fractions, or decimals which either terminate or recur (remember, recurring decimals can be turned into fractions).

Circle all the numbers in this list that are rational numbers.

$\frac{4}{17}$	$\frac{2}{3}$	0.25	π	$\sqrt{11}$	$0.1\dot{7}$	12	$\sqrt{\frac{1}{2}}$	$\sqrt{\frac{1}{25}}$	$\sqrt{16}$

5 The **irrational numbers** include decimals that do not terminate or recur. These include most roots and numbers such as π.

Circle all the numbers in this list that are irrational numbers.

100	2π	$\frac{7}{11}$	$0.\dot{5}9\dot{8}$	$\sqrt{5}$	$\frac{1}{23}$	$\sqrt{0.04}$	$\sqrt{\frac{1}{2}}$	$\frac{3}{19}$	$\sqrt{\frac{1}{49}}$

The **real** numbers include all rational and irrational numbers.

Note:
As well as the **real** numbers, there are numbers that are known as **unreal** or **imaginary** numbers! (Only a pure mathematician could come up with such an idea.) Some of you will meet these in Year 13.

ISBN: 9780170447010

Rounding

- Often we need to round numbers to sensible and/or meaningful values.
- Never round until **after** you have completed your calculations.

Rounding decimals

- The number of decimal places is the number of digits after the decimal point.

Examples:

Number	9	9.0	9.05	9.056	9.0560
Number of decimal places	0	1	2	3	4

Notice that a **0** at the **end** counts as a decimal place.

The process of rounding:
Locate the digit you have to round to. Is the digit to its **right** 5 or more?

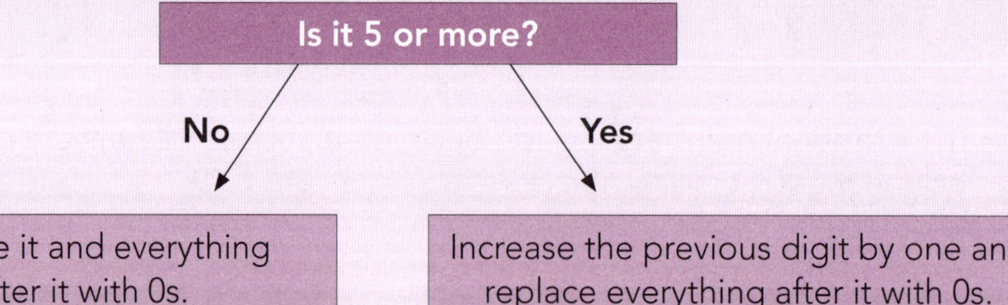

Examples: 1 Round 7.349 to one decimal place.

The digit in the first decimal place is **3**. The digit to its right is **4**.
So 7.349 to one decimal place is 7.3.

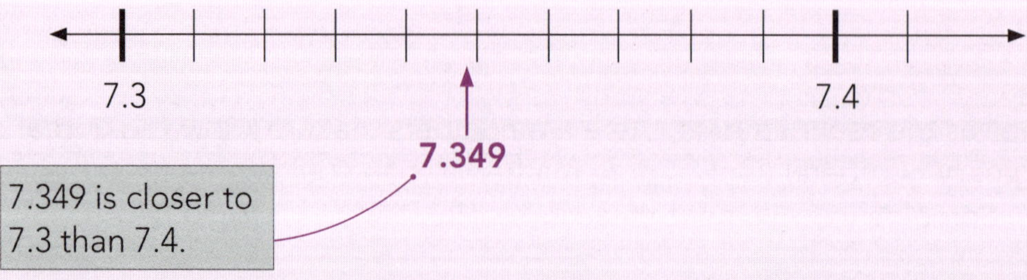

 ISBN: 9780170447010

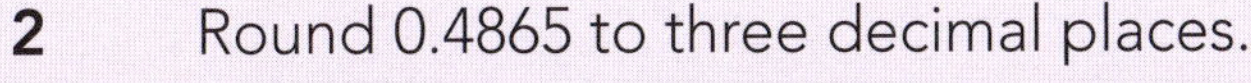

2 Round 0.4865 to three decimal places.

The digit in the third decimal place is **6**. The digit to its right is **5**.
So 0.4865 to the nearest thousandth is 0.487.

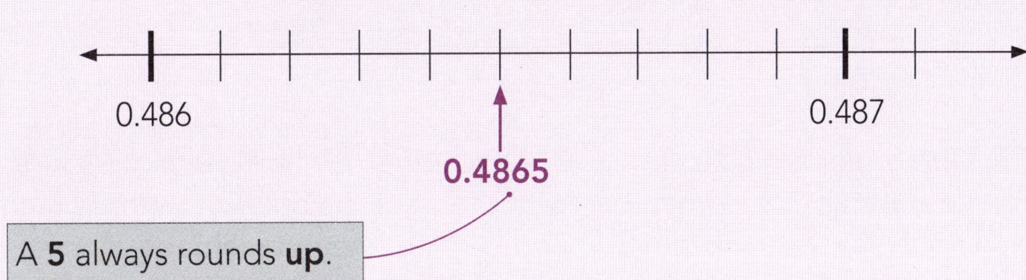

More examples:

	Rounded to the nearest:	Last required digit	Answer
4.15678	1 dp	4.**1**5678	4.2
0.72499	3 dp	0.72**4**99	0.725
11.6957	2 dp	11.6**9**57	11.70
0.59999	4 dp	0.599**9**9	0.6000

Note the 0s at the ends of the last two answers. These are needed to make up the required number of decimal places.

1 Complete the table.

	0 dp	1 dp	2 dp
15.5778			
0.5555			
3.6899			
6.0299			
9.9899			
0.0729			
0.9595			

ISBN: 9780170447010

Answer the following questions.

2 The total land area of New Zealand is 268 021 km^2, of which 31 008 km^2 is in national parks. Calculate the percentage of New Zealand's area that is in national parks. Round your answer to 2 dp.

____

3 In 1893, Kate Sheppard collected 31 872 signatures for her 270-metre-long petition requesting that women be given the right to vote. At that time the female population of New Zealand was 307 509. Calculate the percentage of females that signed the petition. Round your answer to 1 dp.

____

4 A total of 100 444 New Zealanders (including medical staff) participated in the First World War. Of these, 58 014 were killed or wounded. Calculate the percentage of New Zealand participants in the First World War that were killed or wounded. Round your answer to 1 dp.

____

Rounding of roots

Usually when you find a root using your calculator, you will need to round your answer. If you round too early in a calculation, you may not get an accurate result.

Demonstrations:

1 $\sqrt{8} = 2.828$ (3 dp). However, $(2.828)^2 = 7.998$, which is less than 8.

2 $980 \times \sqrt{1.2}$ (rounded to the nearest whole number):

If you find $\sqrt{1.2}$ first: $\sqrt{1.2} = 1.095$ (3 dp)

then: $980 \times 1.095 =$ **1 073** (0 dp)

If you do $980 \times \sqrt{1.2}$ as a single calculation: $\sqrt{1.2} \times 980 =$ **1 074** (0 dp)

Perform the following calculations on your calculator, and round your answers to 1 dp.

5 $6\,789\sqrt{14 - 1.87^3} =$ ______________

6 $\sqrt{2.8 \times 4 - 7} \times \dfrac{56}{0.031} =$ ______________

7 $397\sqrt[3]{800} =$ ______________

8 $\dfrac{\sqrt[5]{16.3 \times 4.9^2}}{0.279} =$ ______________

 ISBN: 9780170447010

Significant figures

Rules for deciding if a digit is significant:

1 All non-zero digits are significant.

2 Zero **is** significant if it is
- between two non-zero digits.
  Example: 15 008 has **5** significant figures.
- at the end of a number that has a decimal point.
  Example: 142.0 has **4** significant figures.

3 Zero **is not** significant if it is
- at the start of a number that is smaller than 1.
  Example: 0.046 has **2** significant figures.
- at the end of a number that has no decimal point.
  Example: 49 100 has **3** significant figures.

Write down the number of significant figures in the following.

1 602 ____________ **2** 620 ____________

3 51 006 ____________ **4** 81.012 ____________

5 710.1 ____________ **6** 5.950 ____________

7 5 950 ____________ **8** 0.00591 ____________

9 8 360 000 ____________ **10** 478 000.0 ____________

11 560 001 ____________ **12** 0.07820 ____________

13 0.0099 ____________ **14** 0.6802 ____________

15 300 ____________ **16** 200.010 ____________

17 10.500 ____________ **18** 0.0753 ____________

ISBN: 9780170447010

Rounding to significant figures

- When asked to round to 2 sf (two significant figures), this means there should be **exactly** two significant figures in the answer.

Locate the digit you have to round to. Is the digit to its **right** 5 or more?

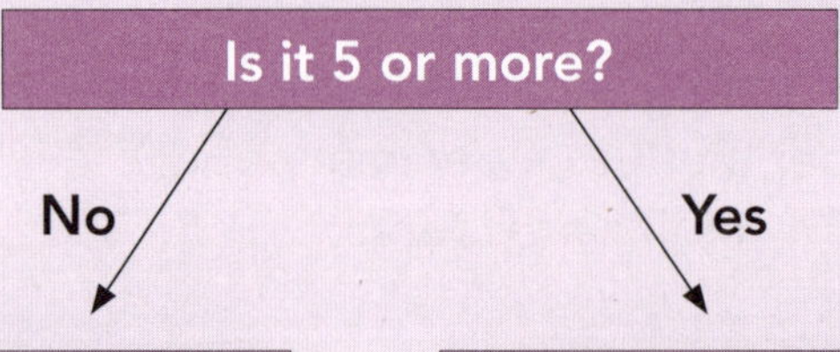

Leave the previous digit alone. | Increase the previous digit by one.

Examples:

1 Round 1.0239 to 3 sf.

The **3** is **not** 5 or more
⇒ leave the 2 alone
∴ 1.0239 = 1.02 (3 sf)

2 Round 1.0259 to 3 sf.

The **5 is** 5 or more
⇒ increase the 2 to 3
∴ 1.0259 = 1.03 (3 sf)

1.0239 is closer to 1.02 than 1.03.

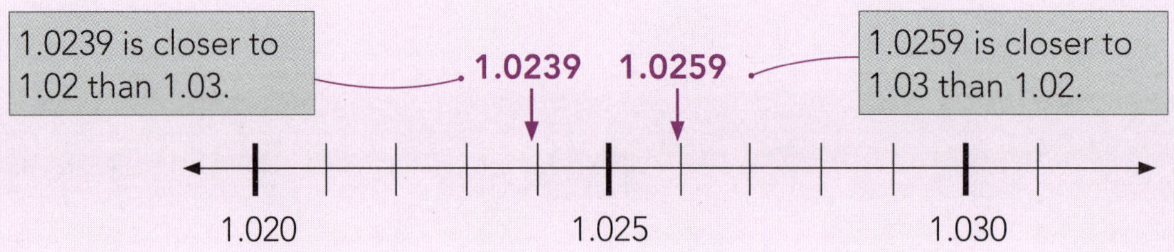

1.0259 is closer to 1.03 than 1.02.

Some more examples:

Unrounded number	Number of significant figures	Rounded number
473 891	2	470 000
1.3680	2	1.4
56.03974	4	56.04
29.5	2	30
599.512	3	600
1 269 845	4	1 270 000
4.697	3	4.70
0.01956	2	0.020
0.040999	4	0.04100

Sometimes you get an answer that looks as though it is rounded to fewer significant figures than you were asked for.

You **must** have the required number of significant figures, so don't omit the 0s at the end.

ISBN: 9780170447010

Round these numbers to 1 sf.

1 455 ____________ **2** 11 478 ____________

3 36.471 ____________ **4** 0.0095 ____________

Round these numbers to 2 sf.

5 4 651 ____________ **6** 119 627 ____________

7 0.0723 ____________ **8** 0.00398 ____________

Round these numbers to 3 sf.

9 291 399 ____________ **10** 3 987 466 ____________

11 5.0097 ____________ **12** 0.04798 ____________

Answer the following questions.

13 10 is the same as 10.0. True or false? ____________
Explain your answer:

____

____

____

14 The table shows the number of bacteria per square centimetre on a range of surfaces. The numbers are given to three significant figures. Calculate the lowest and highest number of bacteria that could be found on each surface. (Remember: most bacteria are harmless, and some are beneficial!)

	Bacteria per cm^2	Lowest number	Highest number
Shopping trolley	21 400		
Keyboard/mouse	12 200		
Mobile phone	1 710		
Remote control	2 640		
Kitchen tap	35 500		
Dish sponge	120 000 000		

ISBN: 9780170447010

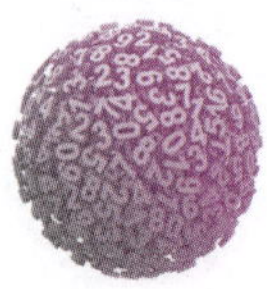

Estimations/approximations

- Sometimes an exact answer isn't necessary, so you can just estimate the answer.
- In order to estimate, round every number to **one significant figure**, and then do the calculations required.
- Don't forget to use BEDMAS.

Example: A list of prices:

This symbol means 'is approximately equal to'.

1.23 kg potatoes @ \$3.99 per kg ≈ \$5.00
0.76 kg carrots @ \$2.49 per kg ≈ \$2.00
0.38 kg mushrooms @ \$10.99 per kg ≈ \$4.00

Round each value to the nearest dollar.

The approximate total is \$11.00.

5 + 2 + 4 = 11

Estimation of roots

- You can estimate the size of a square root by considering the sizes of the perfect squares on either side.

Example: Estimate $\sqrt{20}$.

$4^2 = 16$
$5^2 = 25$

$\therefore \sqrt{20}$ must lie between 4 and 5.

1 Find the values of these square roots by completing the limits column, then choosing the matching value from the box to the right.

	Lower and upper limits	Value
$\sqrt{7}$	2 and 3	2.646
$\sqrt{30}$		
$\sqrt{60}$		
$\sqrt{80}$		

Values to choose from (3 dp)	
5.477	4.676
7.746	6.325
5.702	~~2.646~~
3.464	8.944

Estimate the answers to the following. Do not use a calculator.

2 $2.68 + 3(18.03) =$ ____________

3 $\sqrt{39} + 18.3 - 3.7^2 =$ ____________

4 $\frac{1}{2.1}(\sqrt{66} + 4.5^2) =$ ____________

5 $2.9^3 - 4.3(0.51^2) =$ ____________

6 $0.961^2 \times \frac{\sqrt{106}}{2.19} =$ ____________

7 $2.13 \div 0.22^2 - \sqrt{79.8} =$ ____________

 ISBN: 9780170447010

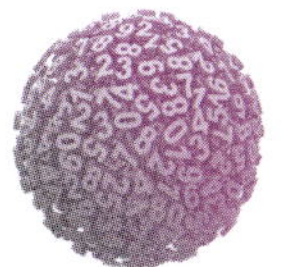

Standard form

- Standard form is a way of writing either very large or very small numbers without writing all the place-holders (0s).
- It is used a lot in science, social science, technology, etc., so it really important that you understand it.
- Standard form is also known as scientific notation.
- Your calculator will sometimes give you answers in standard form.

Powers of 10

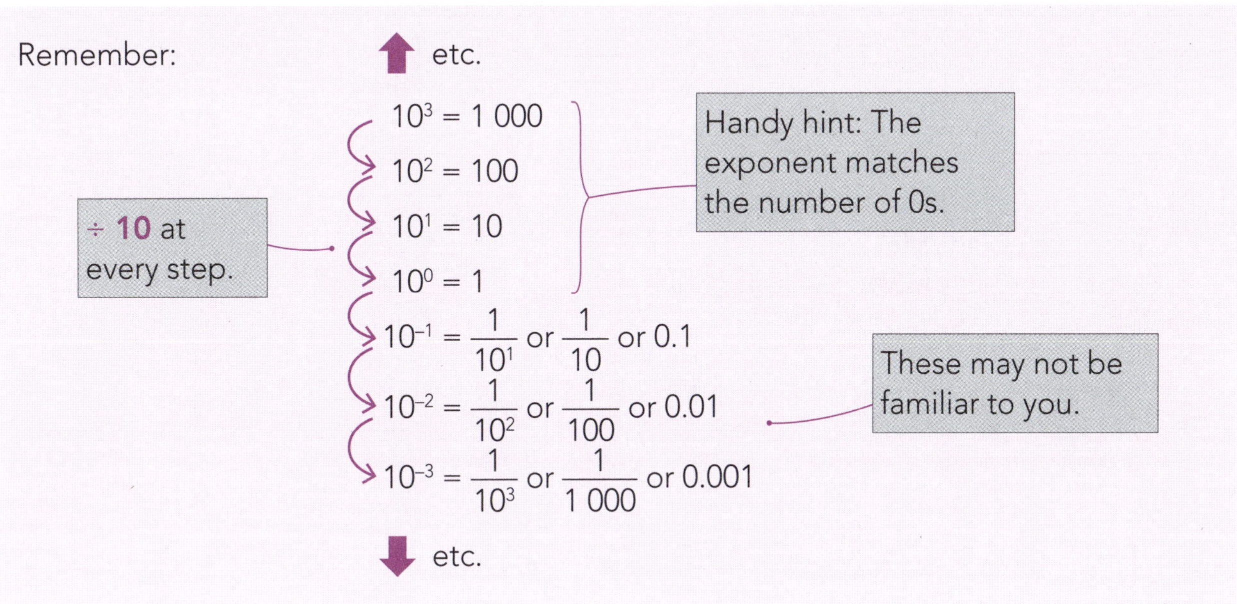

Complete the following table.

Power of 10	Fraction	Whole number or decimal
10^4		
		1
		1 000 000
		0.01
10^{-5}		
	$\frac{1}{1\,000\,000}$	

ISBN: 9780170447010

Numbers in standard form

Converting numbers from standard form to ordinary form

- In standard form, numbers are written in three parts:

A number between 1 and 10 | **x** | **a power of 10**

Examples: **1** $5.16 \times 10^4 = 5\,.\,1\,6\,0\,0$

$= 51\,600$

This means the decimal point shifts **4** places to the **right**.

You must not forget to include the place-keeping **00** before the decimal point.

2 $7.23 \times 10^{-3} = 0\,.\,0\,0\,7\,.\,2\,3$

$= 0.00723$

This means the decimal point shifts **3** places to the **left**.

This is the same as $7.23 \div 1\,000 = 0.00723$.

Convert these numbers to ordinary form without using a calculator.

1 $3.89 \times 10^4 =$ ____________

2 $2.796 \times 10^2 =$ ____________

3 $1.53 \times 10^6 =$ ____________

4 $6.42 \times 10^0 =$ ____________

5 $8.0 \times 10^1 =$ ____________

6 $4.162 \times 10^3 =$ ____________

7 $9.32 \times 10^{-2} =$ ____________

8 $8.012 \times 10^{-1} =$ ____________

9 $8.7 \times 10^{-5} =$ ____________

10 $1.008 \times 10^{-4} =$ ____________

11 $2.0 \times 10^{-6} =$ ____________

12 $7.102 \times 10^{-5} =$ ____________

On your calculator:

Find either an EXP or a $\times 10^x$ button and experiment with whichever you have to discover how it works. Use it to check your answers to numbers **1** to **12**.

 ISBN: 9780170447010

Converting numbers from ordinary form to standard form

Examples:

1 Convert 67 000 to standard form.

Step 1:
Shift the decimal point to the **left** until there is exactly **one** non-zero digit on its left:
(This will give you a number between 1 and 10.)

6. 7 0 0 0. ⇒ **6**.7

Step 2:
Multiply by 10 to the power of however many places the decimal point was moved (**4**):

6.7×10^4

2 Convert 0.0045 to standard form.

Step 1:
Shift the decimal point to the **right** until there is exactly **one** non-zero digit on its left:

0. 0 0 4. 5 ⇒ **4**.5

Step 2:
Multiply by 10 to the **negative** power of however many places the decimal point was moved (**3**):

4.5×10^{-3}

Examples:

Number	Number between 1 and 10	Power of 10	Number in standard form
9 521 000	9.521	6	9.521×10^6
400	4.00	2	4.00×10^2
0.00723	7.23	–3	7.23×10^{-3}
0.2	2	–1	2×10^{-1}

Note: 0.2 has just one significant figure, so it must have one significant figure in standard form.

Write each of the following in standard form.

13 6 300 = ______________________

14 1 498 000 = ______________________

15 90 = ______________________

16 6 = ______________________

17 500 000 = ______________________

18 2.8 = ______________________

19 0.0000085 = ______________________

20 0.0146 = ______________________

ISBN: 9780170447010

Answer the following questions.

21 The human body contains about:

a 1.609×10^5 km of blood vessels. Calculate how many circuits of a 400 m athletics track the blood vessels of a single human body could cover. Write your answer in ordinary form.

b 37.2 trillion cells. A trillion is a million million. Write the number of cells in the human body in standard form.

c 0.2 mg of gold. A gram is 1 000 mg and a kilogram is 1 000 g. Write the number of kg of gold in a human body in standard form.

22 A study has shown that wearing headphones for an hour can increase the bacteria in your ear by 700 times. If the normal number of bacteria in your ear is 2×10^6, how many will there be after wearing headphones for an hour?

23 In 2020, the world population is 7.8 billion (a billion is a thousand million).

a It is estimated that there are 1.4 million ants for every person. Write the estimated number of ants in the world in standard form.

b It is estimated that there are 17 million flies for every person. How many people are there for every fly? Write your answer to 2 sf and in standard form.

24 Lightning strikes the earth 100 times every second. Calculate the number of times lightning strikes the earth during a year. Write your answer to 3 sf and in standard form.

25 The mass of the earth is 5.972×10^{24} kg and the mass of the sun is 1.989×10^{30} kg. What fraction of the sun's mass is that of the earth? Write your answer as a decimal to 1 sf and in standard form.

ISBN: 9780170447010

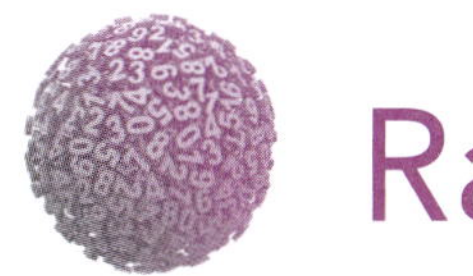

Rates

- Rates are often written using the word 'per'.
- Rates are values with respect to a different unit.
- Examples: the amount ($) paid per hour for babysitting;
  the cost ($) per kilogram of apples;
  the speed of a car in kilometres per hour.

Examples:

1 9 kg of tomatoes cost $25.65. Calculate the cost of 5 kg of tomatoes.

Step 1: Write the information you are given in a brief statement:

9 kg cost **$25.65**

Because you are trying to find a price, put the **price** on the **right**.

Step 2: Underneath write a parallel statement about what you want to know:

9 kg cost **$25.65**

copy ↓

5 kg cost **$25.65** x $\frac{5}{9}$ = $14.25

Multiply by either $\frac{5}{9}$ or $\frac{9}{5}$. Use $\frac{5}{9}$ here because 5 kg will cost **less**.

2 If Marama hires an Orange scooter to get home from town, she can travel at 18 kph and it takes her 7 minutes. How long would it take her to walk home from town at 4 kph?

Step 1: Write the information you are given in a brief statement:

At **18** kph she takes **7 min**

Because you are trying to find a time, put the **time** on the **right**.

Step 2: Underneath write a parallel statement:

At **18** kph she takes **7 min**

copy ↓

At **4** kph she takes **7** x $\frac{18}{4}$ = 31.5 min

Multiply by either $\frac{4}{18}$ or $\frac{18}{4}$. Use $\frac{18}{4}$ here because it will take her **longer** to walk.

ISBN: 9780170447010

Answer the following questions.

1 If Tui walks to school at 4 kph, it takes her 45 minutes. How long would it take her if she skateboards at 9 kph? Round your answer to the nearest minute.

2 Packets of almonds come in two sizes: 150 g for $4.00 and 400 g for $10.50. Which packet is cheaper per kg? Justify your answer.

3 The scale on a map shows that 5 cm = 1 km. An orienteering course is 32.25 cm on the map. How many kilometres is it from start to finish?

4 A speed of one knot is equivalent to a speed of 1.852 kph. If a boat is travelling at 15 kph, what is its speed in knots? Round your answer to 3 sf.

5 It took five people 51 hours to lay pavers in a courtyard. How long would the job have taken if only three people worked on it?

6 One hundred monarch butterflies weigh 28 g. How many monarch butterflies would you get in 18 g? Round your answer sensibly.

7 The tectonic plates under New Zealand move at about 6 cm per year. How far do they move in a week? Round your answer to 3 sf.

8 A bee has to visit 4 000 flowers to make 21 grams of honey. How many flowers would a bee need to visit in order to produce a 500 g jar of honey? Round your answer sensibly.

ISBN: 9780170447010

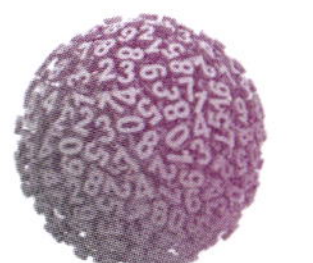

Ratios

Simplifying ratios

- Ratios show how an amount is split into several shares, usually different sizes.
- Before you convert quantities into ratios, both quantities must use the **same units**.
- Ratios are usually given in whole numbers, not decimals or fractions.
- Ratios do **not** have units.
- A **colon** (**:**) is used to separate the two numbers, e.g. 2**:**3 means 'two parts to three parts'.

Examples:

1 Write the ratio $31\frac{1}{2}$:14 in its simplest form.

$31\frac{1}{2}$:14 = 63:28 — Double both parts of the ratio so they are both whole numbers.

63:28 = 9:4 — Divide each of these by their HCF (**7**). 9 and 4 have no common factors.

2 Write the ratio 2.76 L:80 mL in its simplest form.

2.760 L:80 mL = 2760:80 — Change both weights to mL.

2760:80 = 69:2 — Divide each of these by their HCF (**40**). 69 and 2 have no common factors.

Write these ratios in their simplest forms.

1 51:24 = ______

2 10^3:15 = ______

3 60:156 = ______

4 $1\frac{1}{4}$:7 = ______

5 $\frac{3}{4}:\frac{2}{5}$ = ______

6 0.39:1.3 = ______

7 24 kg:60 g = ______
= ______

8 37.5 mL:1 L = ______
= ______

9 25 c:$40 = ______
= ______

10 245 mm:1.4 m = ______
= ______

11 625 m:27 km = ______
= ______

12 1 min 15 s:1 hour = ______
= ______

ISBN: 9780170447010

Using ratios where the total is given

Example: $121.50 needs to be shared between two people in the ratio 4:5.

Step 1: Find the total number of parts by adding the numbers in each share: 4 + 5 = **9**

Step 2: Find the value of one part by dividing the total by the number of parts: $121.50 ÷ **9** = $13.50

Step 3: Multiply the value of one part by each part of the ratio: 4 x $13.50:5 x $13.50

So the ratio of money is $54.00:$67.50.
So one person gets $54 and the other gets $67.50.

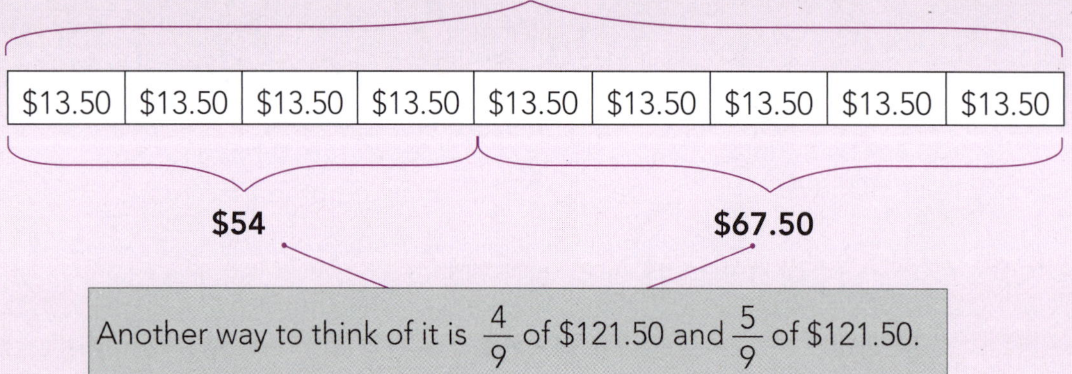

Another way to think of it is $\frac{4}{9}$ of $121.50 and $\frac{5}{9}$ of $121.50.

Note: While the ratio doesn't have units or decimals, your answer could have them.

Share the quantities in the given ratios.

1 $168 in the ratio 3:5

2 $135 in the ratio 7:2

3 1 750 g in the ratio 2:3

4 272 mL in the ratio 13:3

5 36.3 km in the ratio 7:4

6 $186 in the ratio 1:2:3

ISBN: 9780170447010

7 Salad dressing is made from three parts of oil to one part of vinegar. My dressing bottle holds 700 mL, but I need to allow 20 mL for herbs, garlic, etc. How much water and oil will I need?

8 Grandma is moving house, and three cousins shift all her furniture, etc. Tom and Linda spend six hours each, and Mac spends four hours. If Grandma paid them $360 altogether for the job, how much should each of the cousins be paid?

9 Baldwin Street in Dunedin is the steepest residential street in the world. Its steepest section has a gradient of 1:2.86, which means that for every 2.86 m of horizontal distance, it rises 1 m. If the horizontal length of this section is 85.8 m, how much does it rise?

Ratio calculations where one part is given

Examples:

1 Adam and Kara pooled their money to buy a $5 bag of lollies. Adam had $2 and Kara had $3. If they shared them fairly, and Kara got 57 lollies, how many lollies were in the bag?

Step 1: Find the total number of parts by adding the numbers in each share (2 and 3): $2 + 3 = 5$

Step 2: Calculate **the number in each part** by dividing the number given (57) by the number of parts (3) it represents: $57 \div 3 = 19$

Step 3: Multiply the number in each part (19) by the total number of parts (5): $19 \times 5 = 95$

So there were 95 lollies in the bag.

2 Hana and Brendon pooled their money to buy a $9 bag of lollies. Hana had $4 and Brendon had $5. If they shared them fairly, and Hana got 68 lollies, how many lollies did Brendon get?

Step 1: Calculate **the number in each part** by dividing the number given (68) by the number of parts (4) it represents: $68 \div 4 = 17$

Step 2: Multiply the number in each part (17) by the number of parts (5) in the other share: $17 \times 5 = 85$

So Brendon got 85 lollies.

ISBN: 9780170447010

1 a In New Zealand, the ratio of the total number of pet dogs to pet cats is 1:2. If there are 566 000 pet dogs, what is the total number of pet dogs and cats in New Zealand?

b If the ratio of people to dogs is 17:2, how many people would be in New Zealand?

c In New Zealand, the ratio of the annual cost of keeping a cat to the annual cost of keeping a dog is 2:5. On average it costs $1 675 to keep a dog for a year. How much does it cost to keep a cat for a year?

2 The ratio of non-bone tissue to bone tissue is 43:7. If the mass of bone in a person's body is 10.5 kg, calculate the following.

a The mass of their non-bone tissue.

b The total mass.

3 The ratios of the rates of growth of hair, fingernails and toenails are 25:6:3. If fingernails grow at 36 mm per year, calculate the rates of growth of hair and toenails.

4 Sometimes decimals are used in ratios. When this occurs, one of the figures is usually a '1', e.g. the ratio of left-handed males to left-handed females is 1.23:1. This means that for every left-handed female, there are 1.23 left-handed males. If there are 738 left-handed boys at your school, calculate the likely number of left-handed girls.

ISBN: 9780170447010

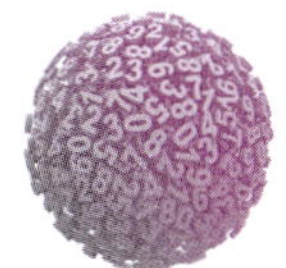

Challenge 5

1 A Californian mite can move at 322 body lengths per second. If a 2 m high (long) human could move at 322 body lengths per second, calculate their speed in

a m per minute: ______

b m per hour: ______

c kph: ______

2 An estimate for the number of stars in the Milky Way is $2.5 \times 10^{11} \pm 1.5 \times 10^{11}$. Write down

a the minimum number from this estimate:

______

______

b the maximum number from this estimate:

______

c It is also estimated that the ratio of trees on earth to the number of stars in the Milky Way is 12:1. Estimate the minimum and maximum number of trees on earth.

Minimum: ______

Maximum: ______

3 There are 7 billion people on earth (a billion is one thousand million) and the human body contains 35 trillion cells (a trillion is one thousand billion). Calculate the ratio of the number of cells in the human body to the number of people on the earth.

______

4 There are more than 100 billion stars in the Milky Way galaxy, and there are over 100 million galaxies in the universe. Write the number of stars in the universe in standard form.

______

5 The human eye blinks 4.2×10^6 times a year. How many times does it blink each day? Round your answer to 4 sf.

______

6 A single hydrogen atom has a diameter of 5.0×10^{-11} mm. A human hair has a diameter of 0.05 mm. Calculate the ratio of the diameter of a human hair to the diameter of a hydrogen atom. Write your answer in standard form.

______

______

ISBN: 9780170447010

Revision 1

1 **a** $-7-(-3)+(-10)=$ ______ **b** $-6 \times -3 \div -10=$ ______

2 What is the lowest common multiple of 9 and 15? ______

3 Write down the highest common factor of 48 and 18: ______

4 Write 76 as the product of prime factors: ______

5 Explain why there are no numbers that are both prime and square.

______

6 I am a triangular number and I am also prime. What am I? ______

7 $6! \div 12=$ ______

8 **a** $(-3)^3=$ ______ **b** $3^{-2}=$ ______

c $\sqrt[3]{-125}=$ ______ **d** $\sqrt[4]{0.0016}=$ ______

e $48-0.5(5-3^2)^3=$ ______ **f** $\frac{\sqrt{100-6^2}}{(-2)^3} \div \frac{1}{2}=$ ______

9 Fill in the empty boxes to make the statements true.

a $\frac{34}{51}=\frac{\square}{60}$ **b** $\frac{31}{7}=\square\frac{\square}{7}$

10 Calculate these.

a $\frac{9}{11}-\frac{3}{4}=$ ______ $=$ ______ **b** $\frac{2}{9}+\frac{5}{6}=$ ______ $=$ ______

c $\frac{4}{7} \times \frac{2}{3}=$ ______ $=$ ______ **d** $\frac{5}{8} \div \frac{2}{5}=$ ______ $=$ ______

e $\sqrt{\frac{4}{25}}=$ ______ **f** $\sqrt[3]{15\frac{5}{8}}=$ ______

11 **a** $\frac{2}{7}$ of $42=$ ______ **b** $2\frac{2}{13}$ of $52=$ ______

ISBN: 9780170447010

12 **a** Hunter planted some chilli seeds. Of those he planted, $\frac{1}{6}$ failed to germinate. Then the dog destroyed a fifth of those that germinated. What fraction of the seeds that he planted survived?

____

b If he sold $\frac{7}{8}$ of his surviving seedlings at the market and was left with three seedlings, how many seeds did he plant?

____

13 **a** Write using words.

602 013 017 = ______________________________

b Write using numerals.

Fifteen million, four thousand and thirty-one = ______________________________

14 Write the values of the purple numerals.

a 102.42**7**: ______________

b 19.6**0**5: ______________

15 Elena's fastest time for the 50 m backstroke was 35.27 seconds. At the school swimming sports she improved her time by nine hundredths of a second. What was her new best time?

____

16 Write the missing decimals on the number line.

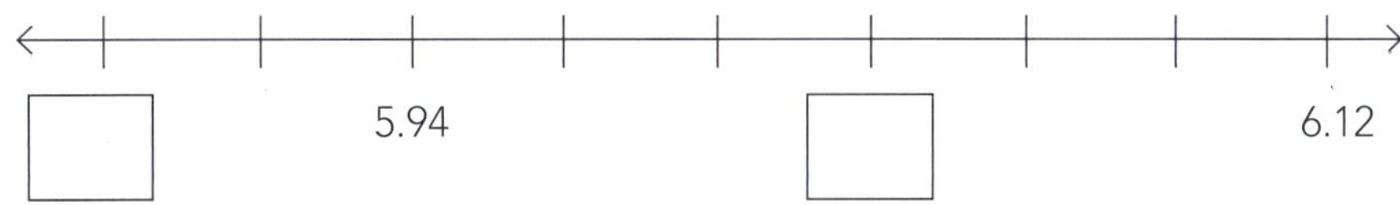

17 Insert an appropriate symbol to make each statement true.

a $\frac{5}{7}$ ☐ $0.\dot{7}$

b $\frac{6}{11}$ ☐ $\frac{11}{20}$

18 Write $1\frac{19}{22}$ as a recurring decimal: ______________________________

19 **a** Write the binary number 100110 as a number in base 10: ______________

b Write 23 as a binary number: ______________________________

ISBN: 9780170447010

20 Convert these values to fill in the gaps.

	Fraction	Fraction over 100	Decimal	Percentage
a				9%
b		$\frac{105}{100}$		
c	$\frac{7}{8}$			

21 Calculate these.

a 0.1% of 48 = ____________ **b** 120% of 95 = ____________

22 **a** Show how $0.\dot{1}\dot{2}$ can be written as a fraction:

____

b Which group of numbers does $0.\dot{1}\dot{2}$ belong to? ____________

23 Humans have about 9 000 taste buds, while dogs have about 1 700. Write the number of taste buds that a dog has as a percentage of the number a human has. Round your answer to 2 dp.

____

24 Charlie's rent increased from $245 to $260 per week. Calculate the percentage increase and round your answer to 1 dp.

____

____

25 One day on earth lasts for 0.8565% of a day on Venus. How long (in earth days) is a day on Venus? Round your answer to 4 sf.

____

____

26 A bumblebee beats its wings 160 times per second. How many beats would it make during an hour of flying? Write your answer in standard form.

____

____

27 It nine students can make up 36 packs of lamingtons in four hours, how many packets can be made up by six students in five hours?

____

____

ISBN: 9780170447010

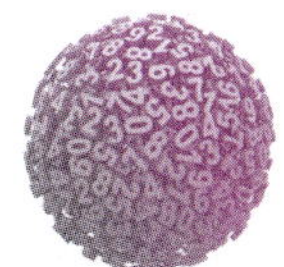

Revision 2

1 **a** $-(-4) - 9 - (-2) =$ ______ **b** $-18 \div -16 \times -3 =$ ______

2 What is the lowest common multiple of 12 and 20? ______

3 Write down the highest common factor of 36 and 16: ______

4 Write 84 as the product of prime factors: ______

5 I am a palindromic cubic number that is less than 500, and I have exactlly four factors. What am I and what are my factors?

______

6 I am a cubic number, and my three smallest factors are 1, 3 and 7. I am between 9 000 and 10 000. What am I? ______

7 $3 \times 5! =$ ______

8 **a** $(-2)^3 =$ ______ **b** $2^{-3} =$ ______

c $\sqrt{1.44} =$ ______ **d** $\sqrt[3]{0.008} =$ ______

e $0.5^2 \times 8 - \frac{18 - 24}{-2} =$ ______ **f** $\frac{\sqrt{7^2 - 13}}{3} - 1 =$ ______

9 Fill in the empty boxes to make the statements true.

a $\frac{57}{76} = \frac{36}{\square}$ **b** $\frac{37}{11} = \square\frac{\square}{11}$

10 Calculate these.

a $\frac{3}{8} + \frac{2}{5} =$ ______
$=$ ______

b $\frac{6}{7} - \frac{3}{4} =$ ______
$=$ ______

c $\frac{2}{9} \times \frac{3}{4} =$ ______
$=$ ______

d $\frac{5}{7} \div \frac{1}{4} =$ ______
$=$ ______

e $\sqrt{\frac{1}{9}} =$ ______ **f** $\sqrt[4]{5\frac{1}{16}} =$ ______

ISBN: 9780170447010

11 **a** $\frac{4}{5}$ of 45 = ____________ **b** $1\frac{7}{15}$ of 75 = ____________

12 **a** There was $\frac{3}{4}$ of a block of chocolate in the pantry. Dad sneaked a sixth of it. What fraction of the original block was left for the rest of the family?

____

b The remainder of the block was shared equally among Mum and four children. If they got four squares each, how many squares were in the block before it was opened?

____

13 **a** Write using words.

40 052 001 = ______________________________

b Write using numerals.

Six hundred and two million, sixteen thousand and five = ____________

14 Write the values of the purple numerals.

a 723.**1**02: ____________ **b** 5.8**2**7: ____________

15 A woodpecker can peck 20 times per second. How many thousandths of a second does it take for it to peck once?

____

16 Write the missing decimals on the number line.

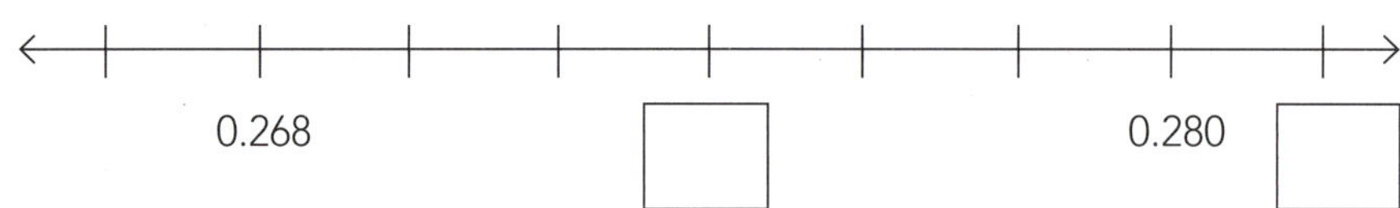

17 Insert an appropriate symbol to make each statement true.

a $\frac{1}{3}$ ☐ $\frac{3}{9}$ **b** 25% ☐ $\frac{1}{5}$

18 Write $\frac{13}{27}$ as a recurring decimal: ______________________________

19 **a** Write the binary number 11101 as a number in base 10: ____________

b Write 17 as a binary number: ______________________________

ISBN: 9780170447010

20 Convert these values to fill in the gaps.

	Fraction	Fraction over 100	Decimal	Percentage
a		$\frac{5}{100}$		
b	$\frac{3}{8}$			
c				2.5%

21 Calculate these.

a 125% of 92 = ____________ **b** 0.1% of 684 = ____________

22 **a** Show how $0.\dot{7}$ can be written as a fraction:

____

b Which group of numbers does π belong to? ____________

23 A giant weta weighs, on average, 70 g. A housefly weighs, on average, 15 mg. Write the weight of a housefly as a percentage of the weight of a giant weta. Round your answer to 3 sf.

____

24 Freddie's pay increased from $18.20 to $19.50 per hour. Calculate the percentage increase, and round your answer to 2 sf.

____

____

25 There are 2 598 960 possible hands in five-card poker. Round this to 3 sf, and write it in standard form.

____

____

26 The ratio of left-handed people to right-handed people is 12:88. If there are 234 left-handed people in a group, how many people would you expect to be right-handed?

____

____

27 If three people can make up 12 kitset chairs in two days, how many chairs could be made up by five people in three days?

____

____

ISBN: 9780170447010

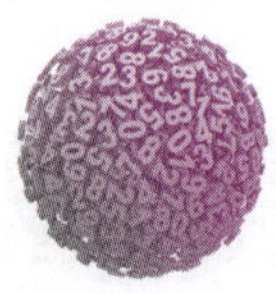

Answers

The language of mathematics (p. 6)

Words to operations (p. 6)

1 –
2 +
3 x
4 –
5 +
6 +
7 ÷
8 +
9 –
10 –
11 +
12 +
13 x
14 –
15 x
16 +
17 ÷
18 –
19 x

Integers (pp. 7–8)

Adding and subtracting (p. 7)

1 1 + 4 – 9 – 3 = –7
2 –2 + 5 – 8 + 13 = 8
3 –7 + 13 – 7 – 2 + 11 = 8
4 5 – 8 – 4 + 6 + 10 – 19 = –10
5 + 9 – 8 + 7 + 6 – 5 = 9
+ 9 + 8 – 7 – 6 + 5 = 9
6 + 9 – 8 – 7 + 6 – 5 = –5
– 9 + 8 + 7 – 6 – 5 = –5

Multiplying and dividing (p. 8)

1 27
2 36
3 –2
4 –8
5 –16
6 12
7 –60
8 $-\frac{1}{2}$

Mixing it up (p. 8)

1 –8°C
2 Second floor
3 $49
4 26 m

Types of numbers (pp. 9–17)

Multiples (p. 9)

1

Number	First five multiples
2	2, 4, 6, 8, 10
11	11, 22, 33, 44, 55
13	13, 26, 39, 52, 65
25	25, 50, 75, 100, 125

2

True or False
True
True
False
True

3 6, 12, 18, 24, **30**
5, 10, 15, 20, 25, **30** LCM is 30
4 9, 18, 27, 36, 45, 54, **63**
7, 14, 21, 28, 35, 42, 49, 56, **63** LCM is 63
5 12, **24**, 36, 48
8, 16, **24**, 32, 40, 48 LCM is 24
6 4, 8, 12, 16, 20, 24, 28, 32, 36, 40, 44, 48, **52**
13, 26, 39, **52** LCM is 52

Factors (p. 10)

1

Number	First five multiples
20	1, 2, 4, 5, 10, 20
18	1, 2, 3, 6, 9, 18
23	1, 23
60	1, 2, 3, 4, 5, 6, 10, 12, 15, 20, 30, 60

2

True or False
True
True
False
False

3 1, 2, **4**, 8
1, 2, **4**, 5, 10, 20 HCF is 4
4 **1**, 2, 7, 14
1, 29 HCF is 1
5 1, 2, **4**, 8, 16
1, 2, **4**, 7, 14, 28 HCF is 4

Mixing it up (p. 11)

1 6 bags, which each contain 6 mints, 5 milkshakes and 8 toffees.
2 a 300 hotdogs
b Packets of sausages: 25
Loaves of bread: 15
Bottles of sauce: 12
3 12 squares, each 6 cm on each edge.
4 a 24 seconds after 10 am.
b 13 times (don't forget they ring together at exactly 10 am)
c 4 minutes and 48 seconds after 10 am.
5 10 has just four factors (1, 2, 5 and 10) whereas 60 has 12 factors (1, 2, 3, 4, 5, 6, 10, 12, 15, 20, 30 and 60). This would make it much easier to work out fractions of a whole.

ISBN: 9780170447010

Prime numbers (pp. 12–14)

1

1	**2**	**3**	4	**5**	6	**7**	8	9	10
11	12	**13**	14	15	16	**17**	18	**19**	20
21	22	**23**	24	25	26	27	28	**29**	30
31	32	33	34	35	36	**37**	38	39	40
41	42	**43**	44	45	46	**47**	48	49	50

2 a $\frac{23}{2}$ = 11.5, and this is not an integral (whole number) answer, so dividing 23 by any other even number (4) would not produce integral answers either.

Similarly, $\frac{23}{3} = 7.\dot{6}$, which is not integral.

There is no point in testing numbers bigger than 4, because $5^2 = 25$, which is bigger than 23.

So, dividing 23 by 2, 3 or 4 doesn't produce an integral answer, so 23 must be prime.

b Try dividing 53 by every prime number up to 7, because $\sqrt{58} = 7.28$. If I use anything bigger than 7, I will be repeating the same calculations.

None of the divisions $\frac{53}{2}, \frac{53}{3}, \frac{53}{5}$ or $\frac{53}{7}$ result in an integer, so 53 must be prime.

c I need to **divide** the number by every **prime** number which is less than the **square root** of the number. If any answers are integers, then the number **is not** prime.

3 $98 = 2 \times 7^2$

4 $81 = 3^4$

5 $90 = 2 \times 3^2 \times 5$

6 $72 = 2^3 \times 3^2$

Investigation

1

			Prime?
$2^2 - 1$	4 – 1	3	✓
$2^3 - 1$	8 – 1	7	✓
$2^4 - 1$	16 – 1	15	×
$2^5 - 1$	32 – 1	31	✓
$2^6 - 1$	64 – 1	63	×
$2^7 - 1$	127 – 1	127	✓
$2^8 - 1$	256 – 1	255	×

2 4 095. It is not prime because 5 is a factor.

3 8 191

4 2 147 483 647

5 $\frac{24\,862\,048}{2}$ sec $= \frac{12\,431\,024}{60}$ minutes

$= \frac{207\,183.73}{60}$ hours

$= \frac{3\,453}{24}$ days

= 144 to the nearest day

6 2, 3, 5, 7, 11, 101, 131, 151, 181, 191

Square numbers (p. 15)

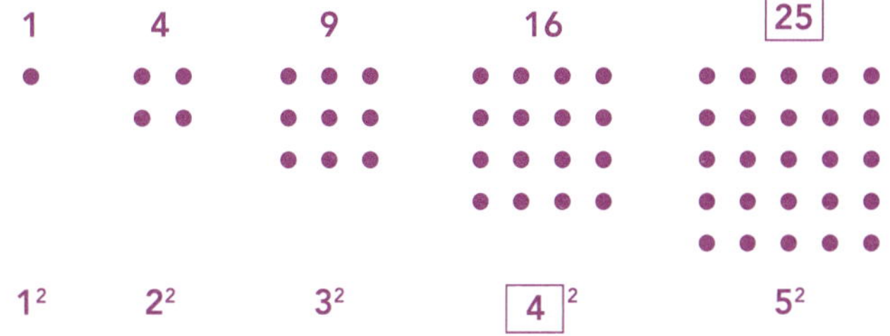

1 36, 49, 64, 81, 100, 121, 144, 169, 196

2 Any two of 169, 196, 961.

3 $36 = 2^2 \times 3^2$. 2^2 and 3^2 are both square numbers, so 36 must also be a square number.

4 $81 = 3^4 = 3^2 \times 3^2$, so 81 must be a square number.

5 $576 = 2^6 \times 3^2 = 2^3 \times 2^3 \times 3^2 = (2^3)^2 \times 3^2$, so 576 is a square number.

6 Sometimes. All squares of whole numbers are bigger than the original number except for 1^2, which is equal to 1.

Cubic numbers (p. 16)

1 216, 343, 512

2 a

Layer	Number of extra cubes needed	Total
Core (dark purple)	1	1
1 (light purple)	$3^3 - 1 = 26$	27
2	$5^3 - 27 = 98$	125
3	$7^3 - 125 = 218$	343
4	$9^3 - 343 = 386$	729

b Layer 6: Needs $11^3 - 729 =$ **602** extra blocks.

Total blocks = 1 331

Layer 7: Need $13^3 - 1\,331 =$ **866** extra blocks.

Total blocks = 2 197

Layer 8: Needs $15^3 - 2\,197 =$ **1 178** extra blocks, which is more than 1 000.

So the maximum number of layers he can make is 7.

Triangular numbers (p. 17)

1 21, 28, 36, 45, 55, 66 2 1, 36

3 Yes. 1 4 1, 3, 6, 55, 66

5 a The answer is a square number.

b

etc.

ISBN: 9780170447010

Weird stuff (p. 18)

1

Row	Sum of the cubes			Square of the sums		
1	1^3	1	**1**	1^2	1^2	**1**
2	$1^3 + 2^3$	1 + 8	**9**	$(1 + 2)^2$	3^2	**9**
3	$1^3 + 2^3 + 3^3$	1 + 8 + 27	**36**	$(1 + 2 + 3)^2$	6^2	**36**
4	$1^3 + 2^3 + 3^3 + 4^3$	1 + 8 + 27 + 64	**100**	$(1 + 2 + 3 + 4)^2$	10^2	**100**
5	$1^3 + 2^3 + 3^3 + 4^3 + 5^3$	1 + 8 + 27 + 64 + 125	**225**	$(1 + 2 + 3 + 4 + 5)^2$	15^2	**225**
6	$1^3 + 2^3 + 3^3 + 4^3 + 5^3 + 6^3$	1 + 8 + 27 + 64 + 125 + 216	**441**	$(1 + 2 + 3 + 4 + 5 + 6)^2$	21^2	**441**

2 a

		First	Next 2	Next 3	Next 4	Next 5
Odd numbers		1	3 5	7 9 11	13 15 17 19	21 23 25 27 29
Sum		1	8	27	64	125
		1^3	2^3	3^3	4^3	5^3
Mean		1	4	9	16	25
		1^2	2^2	3^2	4^2	5^2

b
- The column number is the same as the number of odd numbers in that column.
- The mean of the odd numbers in each column = (column number)^2.
- The sum of the odd numbers = their mean x the number of odd numbers in the column
  = (column number)^2 x column number
  = (column number)^3

Factorials (p. 19)

1 24 **2** 720
3 720 **4** They are the same.
5 6 696 **6** 33 620

Powers (p. 20–21)

1 7^4 **2** -6^3
3 $(-8)^4$ **4** $(-10)^5$
5 100 000 **6** 1
7 0.25 **8** 0.0001
9 125 **10** –0.25
11 –10 000 **12** 10 000
13 –9 **14** 1
15 1 000 000 **16** 0.04
17 16 807 **18** 4 913
19 45 796 **20** –531 441
21 4.826809 **22** 0.015625
23 0.0001 **24** 0.81450625

Puzzle

1 –100 000 000 **2** 1
3 10 000 000 **4** –0.0001
5 –10 000 000 **6** –0.001
7 0.01 **8** 100 000 000
9 0.1 **10** –10 000
11 1 000 000 **12** 0.01

Negative powers (p. 22)

10^4	10 000
10^3	1 000
10^2	100
10^1	10
10^0	1
10^{-1}	$0.1 = \frac{1}{10} = \frac{1}{10^1}$
10^{-2}	$0.01 = \frac{1}{100} = \frac{1}{10^2}$
10^{-3}	$0.001 = \frac{1}{1\,000} = \frac{1}{10^3}$

2^4	16
2^3	8
2^2	4
2^1	2
2^0	1
2^{-1}	$\frac{1}{2} = \frac{1}{2^1}$
2^{-2}	$\frac{1}{4} = \frac{1}{2^2}$
2^{-3}	$\frac{1}{8} = \frac{1}{2^3}$

1 $\frac{1}{49}$ **2** $\frac{1}{1\,000}$
3 $\frac{1}{81}$ **4** $\frac{1}{8}$
5 0.04 **6** 0.0001
7 0.125 **8** 0.25
9 100 **10** 8

Roots (p. 23)

1 9 **2** 5
3 –2 **4** 1 000
5 2 **6** 5
7 –1 **8** –10
9 0.5 **10** 123
11 0.14 **12** –6
13 2.5 **14** $\frac{1}{10}$
15 6 **16** 4

Mixing it up (p. 24)

1 243 **2** 243
3 Yes. 5 **4** 16
5 16 **6** Yes. 4
7 4 096 **8** 4 096
9 Yes. 12 **10** 2^{12}
11 5^8 **12** 11^6
13 $(0.6)^5$ **14** -2^{12}
15 0.1^8 **16** 5^{-2}
17 3^3 **18** 800
19 324 **20** 93 439
21 0.129592 **22** 0.848
23 1 **24** 0.02
25 216

ISBN: 9780170447010

Order of operations (pp. 25–28)

1 4
2 −8
3 −4
4 3
5 −8
6 −7
7 −2
8 68
9 −4.5
10 2
11 $6^2 - 5 \times 4 - 3 - 1 = 12$
12 $4 + 3^2 - 6(5 - 1) = -11$
13 $6 \div 3 \times 1 - 4 + 5^2 = 23$
14 $(3 - 1)^4 - \sqrt{6 + 5 - 2} = 13$
15 $(5\sqrt{4})^2 - 6 \times 3 - 1 = 81$
16 $6^2 - 3\sqrt{5 + 4} + 1 = 28$

Using your calculator (pp. 26–27)

Arctic adventure

The snow piled high on the **sill** casting **beige** light into the **igloo**. He would **ogle** the blocks of ice stacked like **Lego** creating an **isle** of semi-warmth on the ice. The cold crept through the **soles** of his boots, over the Swanndri **logo** on his socks and up his **legs**. **Giles** was so pleased **Ozzie** had agreed to go too, as doing this **solo** would not be much fun. They were both **eligible** for the **zoo** scholarship to study the snow **geese** and **Giles** had to **beg** **Ozzie** to apply. He wasn't sure this was the **bliss** they were promised, alone and cold on this deserted part of the **globe**, harsh **geologies** making everything hard, and freezing cold. The **gloss** on the ice as it sparkled in the sun hid the threat of polar bears that could **seize** them at any time and he hadn't even seen a snow **goose** yet. They would **lie** in their sleeping bags, their heads would **bobble**, the hot food in their **bellies** struggling to warm them. **Giles** checked his sleeping bag was tight. A **loose** drawstring and you could freeze to death. He began to **obsess** about that and told **Ozzie** to check his. They did not hear the muffled squawk from the **bill** of the snow bird or the slush of the snow under the feet of the **big** polar bear as it approached.

Words to calculations (p. 28)

	Calculation	Solution
1	$\frac{12 + 18 + 2 \times 3}{4}$	\$9
2	$\frac{24 \times 4 - 12}{3} - 18$	\$10 more
3	$\frac{3(18 \times 4 - 12)}{2}$	\$90
4	$\frac{18 - 24 + 3 \times 12}{4}$	\$7.50
5	$24 + \frac{3 \times 18}{4} - 2$	\$35.50
6	$\frac{3 \times 12 - 18 - 2}{4}$	4 eggs

Fractions (pp. 29–42)

Numerators and denominators (p. 29)

1

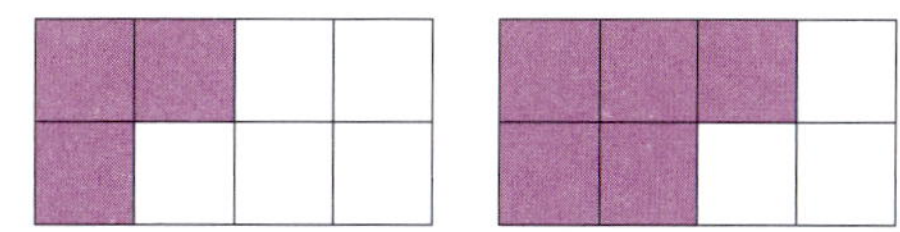

When the **numerator** increases, the size of the shaded section **increases**.

2

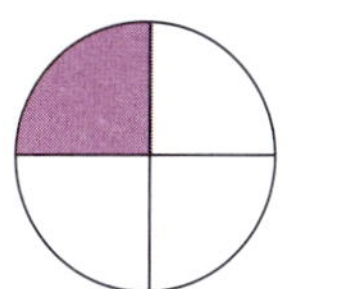

When the **denominator** increases, the size of the shaded section **decreases**.

3

$\frac{1}{17}$	$\frac{2}{17}$	$\frac{5}{17}$	$\frac{11}{17}$	$\frac{12}{17}$	$\frac{15}{17}$	$\frac{20}{17}$

4

$\frac{3}{17}$	$\frac{3}{13}$	$\frac{3}{11}$	$\frac{3}{10}$	$\frac{3}{7}$	$\frac{3}{5}$	$\frac{3}{4}$

Equivalent fractions (p. 30)

1 $\frac{3}{24} = \frac{1}{8}$
2 $\frac{4}{5} = \frac{12}{15}$
3 $\frac{15}{24} = \frac{5}{8}$
4 $\frac{6}{21} = \frac{2}{7}$
5 $\frac{2}{3} = \frac{18}{27}$
6 $\frac{9}{15} = \frac{3}{5}$
7 $\frac{20}{24} = \frac{5}{6}$
8 $\frac{12}{32} = \frac{3}{8}$
9 $\frac{27}{30} = \frac{9}{10}$
10 $\frac{35}{60} = \frac{7}{12}$
11 $\frac{14}{21} = \frac{40}{60} = \frac{18}{27} = \frac{42}{63} = \frac{80}{120} = \frac{2}{3} = \frac{24}{36}$
12 $\frac{27}{45} = \frac{15}{20} = \frac{36}{60} = \frac{15}{25} = \frac{3}{5} = \frac{54}{90} = \frac{18}{30}$
13 $\frac{15}{24} = \frac{60}{96} = \frac{5}{8} = \frac{20}{32} = \frac{10}{16} = \frac{125}{200} = \frac{25}{40}$

Converting between improper and mixed fractions (pp. 31–32)

	Improper fraction		Mixed fraction	
2	$\frac{17}{6}$	Seventeen sixths	$2\frac{5}{6}$	Two and five sixths
3	$\frac{17}{12}$	Seventeen twelfths	$1\frac{5}{12}$	One and five twelfths
4	$\frac{45}{8}$	Forty-five eighths	$5\frac{5}{8}$	Five and five eighths

ISBN: 9780170447010

5 $\frac{19}{7} = \frac{7}{7} + \frac{7}{7} + \frac{5}{7} = 2\frac{5}{7}$

6 $\frac{14}{3} = \frac{3}{3} + \frac{3}{3} + \frac{3}{3} + \frac{3}{3} + \frac{2}{3} = 4\frac{2}{3}$

7 $5\frac{1}{6}$ 8 $3\frac{5}{8}$

9 $2\frac{3}{4}$ 10 $2\frac{2}{9}$

11 $6\frac{3}{5}$ 12 $2\frac{6}{11}$

13 $7\frac{3}{7}$ 14 $5\frac{18}{25}$

15 $\frac{29}{9}$ 16 $\frac{28}{15}$

17 $\frac{25}{11}$ 18 $\frac{38}{7}$

19 $\frac{45}{4}$ 20 $\frac{17}{6}$

21 $\frac{69}{20}$ 22 $\frac{49}{4}$

Adding and subtracting fractions (pp. 33–34)

1 $\frac{5}{7}$ 2 $\frac{7}{8}$

3 $\frac{5}{6}$ 4 $\frac{1}{18}$

5 $\frac{13}{35}$ 6 $\frac{23}{28}$

7 $1\frac{9}{20}$ 8 $\frac{25}{56}$

9 $1\frac{17}{44}$ 10 $1\frac{13}{60}$

11 $1\frac{97}{100}$ 12 $3\frac{3}{44}$

Mixing it up (p. 34)

1 $\frac{199}{200}$ 2 $\frac{1}{4}$

3 $\frac{3}{7}$ 4 $\frac{3}{4}$

Multiplying fractions (p. 35)

1 $\frac{8}{15}$ 2 $\frac{5}{9}$

3 $\frac{5}{36}$ 4 $\frac{6}{11}$

5 $3\frac{1}{3}$ 6 $2\frac{3}{5}$

7 $12\frac{9}{28}$ 8 $45\frac{3}{8}$

9 $1\frac{2}{3}$ 10 $15\frac{21}{100}$

Dividing fractions (pp. 36–37)

1 $\frac{13}{6}$ 2 $\frac{25}{17}$

3 $\frac{6}{17}$ 4 $\frac{7}{65}$

5 $\frac{1}{37}$ 6 $\frac{3}{317}$

7 $\frac{7}{12}$ 8 2

9 $1\frac{4}{5}$ 10 $1\frac{1}{2}$

11 $\frac{2}{3}$ 12 12

13 $1\frac{1}{2}$ 14 1

15 $\frac{5}{6}$ 16 2

Challenge 1 (p. 38)

1 a 84 pieces b $\frac{7}{8}$

c $\frac{7}{24}$

Combining roots and fractions (p. 38)

1 $\frac{1}{3}$ 2 $\frac{5}{6}$

3 $\frac{7}{4}$ 4 $1\frac{3}{7}$

5 $\frac{2}{3}$ 6 $\frac{2}{3}$

Ordering and comparing fractions (pp. 39–40)

Ordering fractions

1

$\frac{5}{6}$	$\frac{7}{12}$	$\frac{3}{4}$	$\frac{1}{2}$	$\frac{5}{8}$	$\frac{2}{3}$	$\frac{5}{12}$	$\frac{7}{8}$
$\frac{20}{24}$	$\frac{14}{24}$	$\frac{18}{24}$	$\frac{12}{24}$	$\frac{15}{24}$	$\frac{16}{24}$	$\frac{10}{24}$	$\frac{21}{24}$

Smallest Largest

$\frac{5}{12}$	$\frac{1}{2}$	$\frac{7}{12}$	$\frac{5}{8}$	$\frac{2}{3}$	$\frac{3}{4}$	$\frac{5}{6}$	$\frac{7}{8}$

ISBN: 9780170447010

2

$\frac{7}{10}$	$\frac{5}{6}$	$\frac{2}{3}$	$\frac{4}{5}$	$\frac{3}{4}$	$\frac{7}{12}$	$\frac{13}{20}$	$\frac{8}{15}$
$\frac{42}{60}$	$\frac{50}{60}$	$\frac{40}{60}$	$\frac{48}{60}$	$\frac{45}{60}$	$\frac{35}{60}$	$\frac{39}{60}$	$\frac{32}{60}$

Smallest Largest

$\frac{8}{15}$	$\frac{7}{12}$	$\frac{13}{20}$	$\frac{2}{3}$	$\frac{7}{10}$	$\frac{3}{4}$	$\frac{4}{5}$	$\frac{5}{6}$

3

$\frac{1}{4}$	$\frac{2}{7}$	$\frac{5}{14}$	$\frac{3}{7}$	$\frac{11}{28}$	$\frac{3}{14}$	$\frac{3}{8}$	$\frac{1}{2}$
$\frac{14}{56}$	$\frac{16}{56}$	$\frac{20}{56}$	$\frac{24}{56}$	$\frac{22}{56}$	$\frac{12}{56}$	$\frac{21}{56}$	$\frac{28}{56}$

Smallest Largest

$\frac{3}{14}$	$\frac{1}{4}$	$\frac{2}{7}$	$\frac{5}{14}$	$\frac{3}{8}$	$\frac{11}{28}$	$\frac{3}{7}$	$\frac{1}{2}$

Comparing fractions

1 $>$ 2 $<$ 3 $>$
4 $<$ 5 $>$ 6 $<$

7 $\frac{2}{3} < \frac{5}{7}$; $\frac{14}{21}$ $\frac{15}{21}$

8 $\frac{3}{4} < \frac{7}{9}$; $\frac{27}{36}$ $\frac{28}{36}$

9 $\frac{7}{8} > \frac{6}{7}$; $\frac{49}{56}$ $\frac{48}{56}$

10 $\frac{2}{7} > \frac{3}{11}$; $\frac{22}{77}$ $\frac{21}{77}$

11 $\frac{7}{12} > \frac{4}{7}$; $\frac{49}{84}$ $\frac{48}{84}$

12 $\frac{13}{20} < \frac{2}{3}$; $\frac{39}{60}$ $\frac{40}{60}$

Fractions of a quantity (p. 41)

1 8
2 36
3 $10\frac{1}{2}$
4 $20\frac{5}{6}$
5 $73\frac{1}{3}$
6 $25\frac{1}{12}$
7 21
8 287 tickets
9 Those in single rooms: $\frac{1}{5}$; $108

Those in double rooms: $\frac{3}{20}$; $81

Mixing it up (p. 42)

1 a $\frac{2}{15}$ each

b Mel ate $\frac{2}{3} \times \frac{1}{4} = \frac{1}{6}$ pizza

c Remaining pizza $= \frac{2}{3} - \frac{1}{6} = \frac{1}{2}$

d $\frac{1}{8}$ each

e $\frac{1}{6} - \frac{1}{8} = \frac{1}{24}$ pizza

2 Yellow courgettes: $\frac{8}{33}$; 16

Green courgettes: $\frac{10}{33}$; 20

Yellow scallopini: $\frac{7}{33}$; 14

Green scallopini: $\frac{5}{33}$; 10

Decimals (pp. 43–55)

Place value (pp. 43–44)

		Number	Words
1	259 176	50 000	Fifty thousand
2	318 627 054	10 000 000	Ten million
3	721 469 123	400 000	Four hundred thousand
4	123 456 980	6 000	Six thousand

		Decimal	Fraction	Words
5	0.192	0.1	$\frac{1}{10}$ or $\frac{100}{1\,000}$	One tenth or one hundred thousandths
6	0.163	0.003	$\frac{3}{1\,000}$	Three thousandths
7	24.057	0.05	$\frac{5}{100}$ or $\frac{50}{1\,000}$	Five hundredths or fifty thousandths

8 Forty-one million, seven hundred and sixty-two thousand, three hundred and ninety-one.
9 Thirty thousand and seventeen.
10 One hundred and eight million, forty-five thousand and six.
11 Forty million, two thousand and thirteen.
12 12 002 093
13 70.018
14 13 027.004
15 12 306 000.05

ISBN: 9780170447010

Decimals on number lines (pp. 45–46)

1
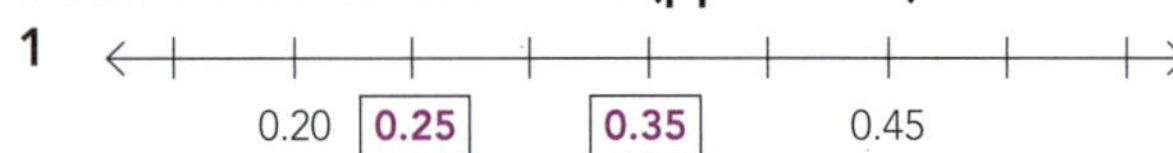

Size of gap $= \frac{0.25}{5} = 0.05$

2

Size of gap $= \frac{0.12}{6} = 0.02$

3

7.03 | 7.09 | 7.18 | 7.27

Size of gap $= \frac{0.15}{5} = 0.03$

4

2.315 | 2.345 | 2.390 | 2.420

Size of gap $= \frac{0.075}{5} = 0.015$

5
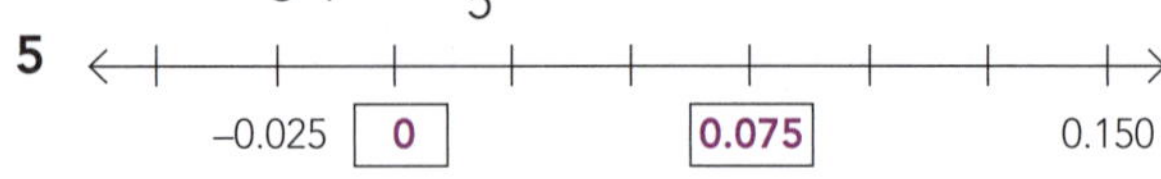

Size of gap $= \frac{0.175}{7} = 0.025$

6
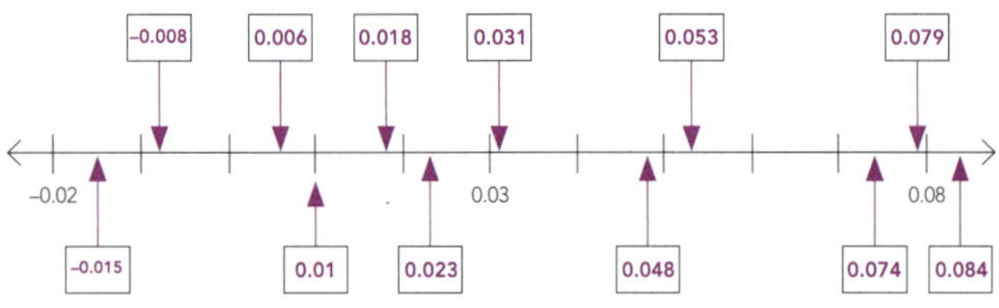

Challenge 2 (p. 46)

1
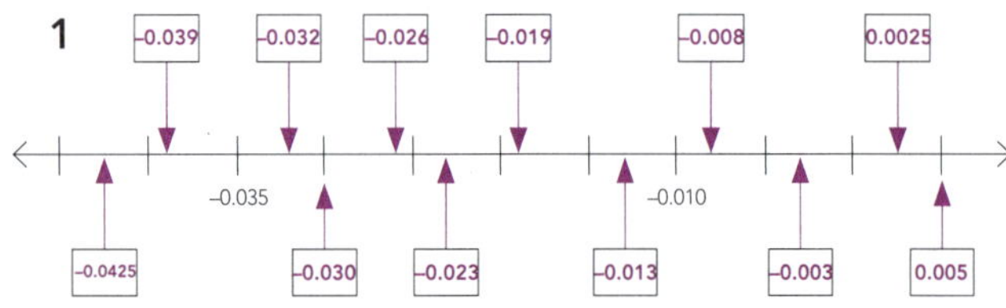

Comparing decimals (p. 47)

1 53.101 < 53.110
2 0.2797 > 0.2779
3 1.2300 = 1.230
4 454.99 < 454.100
5 19.1919 < 19.1920
6 8.51499 > 8.5149
7 0.221
8 14.011
9 26.165
10 9.530
11 9.4261
12 5.0055, 5.0500, 5.0505, 5.5050
13 0.1010, 0.1011, 0.1101, 0.1110

Recurring decimals (p. 48)

1 0.22222…
2 0.818181…
3 0.605605605…
4 0.3498749874987…
5 $0.\dot{4}\dot{9}$
6 $0.\dot{3}4\dot{9}$
7 $0.000\dot{6}$
8 $0.81\dot{5}1\dot{2}$
9 $0.\dot{4}$
10 $0.\dot{4}\dot{5}$
11 $6.5\dot{3}$
12 $10.\dot{2}9\dot{6}$

Turning decimals into fractions (p. 49)

1 $\frac{11}{50}$
2 $\frac{1}{8}$
3 $2\frac{7}{50}$
4 $10\frac{11}{20}$
5 $7\frac{16}{25}$
6 $\frac{31}{200}$
7 $6\frac{17}{125}$
8 $\frac{137}{1250}$

Turning recurring decimals into fractions (pp. 50–51)

1 $\frac{2}{9}$
2 $\frac{5}{33}$
3 $\frac{10}{11}$
4 $\frac{14}{27}$
5 $\frac{26}{27}$
6 $\frac{5}{37}$

7 a

$$x = 0.\dot{1}4285\dot{7}$$
$$1\,000\,000x = 142\,857.\dot{1}4285\dot{7}$$
$$999\,999x = 142\,857$$
$$x = \frac{142\,857}{999\,999} = \frac{1}{7}$$

b

Fraction	Decimal
$\frac{1}{7}$	$0.\dot{1}4285\dot{7}$
$\frac{2}{7}$	$0.\dot{2}8571\dot{4}$
$\frac{3}{7}$	$0.\dot{4}2857\dot{1}$

c

Fraction	Decimal
$\frac{4}{7}$	$0.\dot{5}7142\dot{8}$
$\frac{5}{7}$	$0.\dot{7}1428\dot{5}$
$\frac{6}{7}$	$0.\dot{8}5714\dot{2}$

ISBN: 9780170447010

Challenge 3 (pp. 52–55)

Numbers in base 2 (pp. 52–55)

1

Number in base 2	Number in base 10
11	3
110	6
1000	8
10111	23
100100	36
111011	59

2 7
3 14
4 19
5 64
6 25
7 49
8 9.5
9 4.25
10 13.75
11 0.875
12 1100
13 10001
14 11101
15 100011
16 111100.1
17 1100100.11
18

Mersenne prime	Base 10	Base 2
$2^2 - 1$	3	11
$2^3 - 1$	7	111
$2^5 - 1$	31	11111
$2^7 - 1$	127	1111111
$2^{11} - 1$	2047	11111111111

19 They consist of only ones, no zeros.
20 2^n will always take the form 10, 100, 1000, 10000, etc. Subtracting one from any of these will result in binary numbers consisting of only ones.

Percentages (pp. 56–65)

Converting between decimals and percentages (p. 56)

1 21%
2 6.49%
3 0.75%
4 304%
5 0.71
6 0.048
7 0.006
8 2.73

Converting between fractions and percentages (p. 57)

	Fraction	Decimal	Percentage
1	$\frac{3}{20}$	0.15	15%
2	$\frac{7}{25}$	0.28	28%
3	$\frac{3}{8}$	0.375	37.5%
4	$\frac{123}{500}$	0.246	24.6%
5	$1\frac{3}{4}$	1.75	175%
6	$\frac{5}{8}$	0.625	62.5%
7	$2\frac{3}{5}$	2.6	260%
8	$\frac{1}{200}$	0.005	0.5%

Challenge 4 (p. 58)

1

$\frac{2}{7}$	27.5%	$0.28\dot{3}$	$\frac{4}{15}$	29%	$\frac{5}{17}$	0.285	$\frac{5}{18}$
0.2857	0.275	$0.28\dot{3}$	$0.2\dot{6}$	0.29	0.2941	0.285	$0.2\dot{7}$

Smallest → Largest

$\frac{4}{15}$	27.5%	$\frac{5}{18}$	$0.28\dot{3}$	0.285	$\frac{2}{7}$	29%	$\frac{5}{17}$

2

$0.708\dot{3}$	$\frac{22}{31}$	$0.\dot{7}\dot{2}$	$\frac{19}{27}$	0.71	72.5%	$\frac{18}{25}$	70.5%
$0.708\dot{3}$	0.7097	$0.\dot{7}\dot{2}$	$0.70\dot{3}$	0.71	0.725	0.72	0.705

Smallest → Largest

$\frac{19}{27}$	70.5%	$0.708\dot{3}$	$\frac{22}{31}$	0.71	$\frac{18}{25}$	$0.\dot{7}\dot{2}$	72.5%

3

$0.04\dot{5}$	4.5%	$\frac{2}{37}$	0.05	$\frac{1}{21}$	$\frac{3}{65}$	$0.0\dot{5}$	5.4%
$0.04\dot{5}$	0.045	$0.\dot{0}5\dot{4}$	0.05	0.0476	0.0462	$0.0\dot{5}$	0.054

Smallest → Largest

4.5%	$0.04\dot{5}$	$\frac{3}{65}$	$\frac{1}{21}$	0.05	5.4%	$\frac{2}{37}$	$0.0\dot{5}$

4

$1.\dot{1}\dot{5}$	$1\frac{3}{20}$	$1.\dot{1}6\dot{2}$	114.9%	$\frac{7}{6}$	1.1515	$1\frac{4}{27}$	115.6%
$1.\dot{1}\dot{5}$	1.15	$1.\dot{1}6\dot{2}$	1.149	$1.1\dot{6}$	1.1515	$1.\dot{1}4\dot{8}$	1.156

Smallest → Largest

$1\frac{4}{27}$	114.9%	$1\frac{3}{20}$	1.1515	$1.\dot{1}\dot{5}$	115.6%	$1.\dot{1}6\dot{2}$	$\frac{7}{6}$

Calculating percentages (p. 59)

1 25%
2 80%
3 2.5%
4 1.45%
5 36%
6 12.5%
7 96%
8 26.5%
9 12.5%
10 80.95%

ISBN: 9780170447010

Finding percentages of amounts (pp. 60–61)

1 9
2 18
3 3.5
4 264
5 25.92
6 693
7 270
8 3 500
9 66 people
10 18 hours
11 0.13668 kg

Mixing it up (p. 61)

1 753 000 000
2 a $26.\dot{6}\%$ b $18.\dot{6}$ kg
3 $0.1\dot{6}\%$
4

	kg methane produced per year	as a % of the methane produced by a cow
Human	0.12	0.1%
Pig	1.5	1.25%
Sheep	8	$6.\dot{6}$

Increasing by an amount (p. 62)

1 69
2 42
3 $630
4 540 g
5 91.8 kg
6 86.25 km
7 $1 792
8 8.208 t
9 1 272
10 $18.90
11 654 mL (That's why a glass bottle will break)
12 8.961 L

Decreasing by an amount (p. 63)

1 72
2 99.2
3 $544
4 300 g
5 85.5 kg
6 84.48 km
7 $848.75
8 23.52 t
9 $338 100
10 a $106.25 b $83.30
11 1 008

Finding a percentage increase or decrease (p. 64)

1 20% increase
2 35% decrease
3 15% increase
4 12.5% decrease
5 4% increase
6 5% decrease
7 6% increase
8 2% increase
9 12.5% decrease
10 2.5% increase

Mixing it up (p. 65)

1 $632.50
2 $160
3 The item would normally sell for $115, but you can buy it for $100.

∴ You pay $\frac{100}{115}$ x 100% = 87% of the normal price.
This represents a saving of about 13%, not 15%.

4
Start:

Blue	Red
99%	1%
198 marbles	2 marbles

Finish:

Blue	Red
98%	2%
98 marbles	2 marbles

∴ She needs to remove 100 blue marbles, so there will be 100 marbles in the jar.

5
Start:

Water	Plum
85%	15%
8.5 kg	1.5 kg

Finish:

Water	Plum
25%	75%
0.5 kg	1.5 kg

∴ The dehydrated weight will be 2 kg.

Groups of numbers (pp. 66–67)

1 Natural (or counting) numbers: 1, 2, 3, 4, 5, 6, 7, 8, 9,10
2 Whole numbers (natural numbers and 0): 0, 1, 2, 3, 4, 5, 6, 7, 8, 9
3 Integers: –5, –4, –3, –2, –1, 0, 1, 2, 3, 4, 5
4 Rational numbers:

$\frac{4}{17}$	$\frac{2}{3}$	0.25	π	$\sqrt{11}$	$0.1\dot{7}$	12	$\sqrt{\frac{1}{2}}$	$\sqrt{\frac{1}{25}}$	$\sqrt{16}$

5 Irrational numbers:

100	2π	$\frac{7}{11}$	$0.\dot{5}9\dot{8}$	$\sqrt{5}$	$\frac{1}{23}$	$\sqrt{0.04}$	$\sqrt{\frac{1}{2}}$	$\frac{3}{19}$	$\sqrt{\frac{1}{49}}$

Rounding (pp. 68–73)

Rounding decimals (pp. 68–70)

1

	0 dp	1 dp	2 dp
15.5778	16	15.6	15.58
0.5555	1	0.6	0.56
3.6899	4	3.7	3.69
6.0299	6	6.0	6.03
9.9899	10	10.0	9.99
0.0729	0	0.1	0.07
0.9595	1	1.0	0.96

 ISBN: 9780170447010

2 11.57%
3 10.4% (However, only women over 21 could sign the petition, and the female population figure includes females of all ages.)
4 57.8%
5 18 543.8
6 3 702.1
7 3 685.4
8 11.8

Significant figures (p. 71)

1 3
2 2
3 5
4 5
5 4
6 4
7 3
8 3
9 3
10 7
11 6
12 4
13 2
14 4
15 1
16 6
17 5
18 3

Rounding to significant figures (pp. 72–73)

1 500
2 10 000
3 40
4 0.01
5 4 700
6 120 000
7 0.072
8 0.0040
9 291 000
10 3 990 000
11 5.01
12 0.0480
13 10 could mean 10.0, but if it had been rounded to 0 dp or 1 sf, it could also mean any number between 9.50 and $10.4\dot{9}$.
10.0, if it had been rounded to 3 sf, could mean anything between 9.50 and $10.04\dot{9}$. This is a much narrower band of values.
14

	Bacteria per cm^2	Lowest number	Highest number
Shopping trolley	21 400	21 350	21 449
Keyboard/ mouse	12 200	12 150	12 249
Mobile phone	1 710	1 705	1 714
Remote control	2 640	2 635	2 644
Dish sponge	120 000 000	119 500 000	120 499 999

Estimations/approximations (p. 74)

Estimation of roots (p. 74)

1

	Lower and upper limits	Value
$\sqrt{7}$	2 and 3	2.646
$\sqrt{30}$	5 and 6	5.477
$\sqrt{60}$	7 and 8	7.746
$\sqrt{80}$	8 and 9	8.944

You may get different answers for the following. If so, discuss them with your teacher.

2 63
3 20
4 14
5 26
6 5
7 42

Standard form (p. 75–78)

Powers of 10 (p. 75)

Power of 10	Fraction	Whole number or decimal
10^4		10 000
10^0		1
10^6		1 000 000
10^{-2}	$\frac{1}{100}$	0.01
10^{-5}	$\frac{1}{100\,000}$	0.00001
10^{-6}	$\frac{1}{1\,000\,000}$	0.000001

Numbers in standard form (pp. 76–78)

1 38 900
2 279.6
3 1 530 000
4 6.42
5 80
6 4 162
7 0.0932
8 0.8012
9 0.000087
10 0.0001008
11 0.0000020
12 0.00007102
13 6.3×10^3
14 1.498×10^6
15 9.0×10^1
16 6×10^0
17 5.0×10^5
18 2.8×10^0
19 8.5×10^{-6}
20 1.46×10^{-2}
21 a 40 225
b 3.72×10^{13}
c 2.0×10^{-7}
22 1.4×10^9
23 a 1.092×10^{16}
b 5.9×10^{-8}
24 3.15×10^9
25 3.0×10^{-6}

Rates (pp. 79–80)

1 20 minutes
2 150 g packet costs $\$26.\dot{6}$ per kg.
400 g packet costs $26.25 per kg.
So the 400 g packet is cheaper.
3 6.45 km
4 8.10 knots
5 85 hours
6 64 (round to the nearest whole number)
7 0.115 cm
8 95 238 flowers

ISBN: 9780170447010

Ratios (pp. 81–84)

Simplifying ratios (p. 81)

1	17:8	2	200:3
3	5:13	4	5:28
5	15:8	6	3:10
7	400:1	8	3:80
9	1:160	10	7:40
11	5:216	12	1:48

Using ratios where the total is given (pp. 82–83)

1 $63:$105   2 $105:$30
3 700 g:1050 g   4 221 mL:51 mL
5 23.1 km:13.2 km   6 $31:$62:$93
7 510 mL oil and 170 mL vinegar.
8 Tom and Linda should get $135 each, and Mac should get $90.
9 30 m

Ratio calculations where one part is given (pp. 83–84)

1 a 1 698 000   b 4 811 000
  c $670
2 a 64.5 kg   b 75 kg
3 Hair grows at 150 mm per year. Toenails grow at 18 mm per year.
4 600

Challenge 5 (p. 85)

1 a 38 640 m per minute
  b 2 318 400 m per hour
  c 2 318.4 kph
2 a 1.0×10^{11} b 4×10^{11}
  c Minimum: 1.2×10^{12}
  Maximum: 4.8×10^{12}
3 5 000:1   4 1×10^{19}
5 11 510   6 1.0×10^{9}:1

Revision 1 (pp. 86–88)

1 a −14   b −1.8
2 45   3 6
4 2 x 2 x 19
5 A square number is a product of two integers, so it has at least two factors other than 1. One is a square number but it is not prime ∴ there are no prime square numbers.
6 3   7 60
8 a −27   b $\frac{1}{9}$
  c −5   d 0.2
  e 80   f −2
9 a $\frac{34}{51} = \frac{40}{60}$ b $\frac{31}{7} = 4\frac{3}{7}$
10 a $\frac{3}{44}$ b $1\frac{1}{18}$
  c $\frac{8}{21}$ d $1\frac{9}{16}$
  e $\frac{2}{5}$ f $2\frac{1}{2}$
11 a 12   b 112
12 a $\frac{2}{3}$ b 36
13 a Six hundred and two million, thirteen thousand and seventeen
  b 15 004 031
14 a seven thousandths
  b zero hundredths
15 35.18 seconds
16

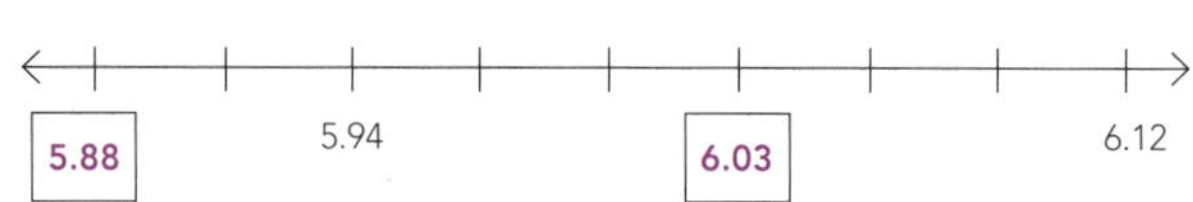

17 a $\frac{5}{7} < 0.\dot{7}$ b $\frac{6}{11} < \frac{11}{20}$
18 $1.\dot{8}\dot{6}\dot{3}$
19 a 38   b 10111
20

	Fraction	Fraction over 100	Decimal	Percentage
a	$\frac{9}{100}$	$\frac{9}{100}$	0.09	9%
b	$\frac{21}{20}$	$\frac{105}{100}$	1.05	105
c	$\frac{7}{8}$	$\frac{87.5}{100}$	0.875	87.5

21 a 0.048   b 114
22 a
$$x = 0.\dot{1}\dot{2}$$
$$100x = 12.\dot{1}\dot{2}$$
$$99x = 12$$
$$x = \frac{12}{99}$$
  b Rational numbers
23 18.89%
24 6.1%
25 116.8 days
26 5.76×10^{5}
27 30 packs

ISBN: 9780170447010

Revision 2 (pp. 89–91)

1 a -3 b -3.375
2 60
3 4
4 $2 \times 2 \times 3 \times 7$
5 343. Factors: 1, 7, 49, 343.
6 9 261
7 360
8 a -8 b $\frac{1}{8}$
c 1.2 d 0.2
e -1 f 1
9 a $\frac{57}{76} = \frac{36}{48}$ b $\frac{37}{11} = 3\frac{4}{11}$
10 a $\frac{31}{40}$ b $\frac{3}{28}$
c $\frac{1}{6}$ d $2\frac{6}{7}$
e $\frac{1}{3}$ f $1\frac{1}{2}$
11 a 36 b 110
12 a $\frac{5}{8}$ b 32 squares
13 a Forty million, fifty-two thousand and one
b 602 016 005
14 a One tenth
b Two hundredths
15 50
16

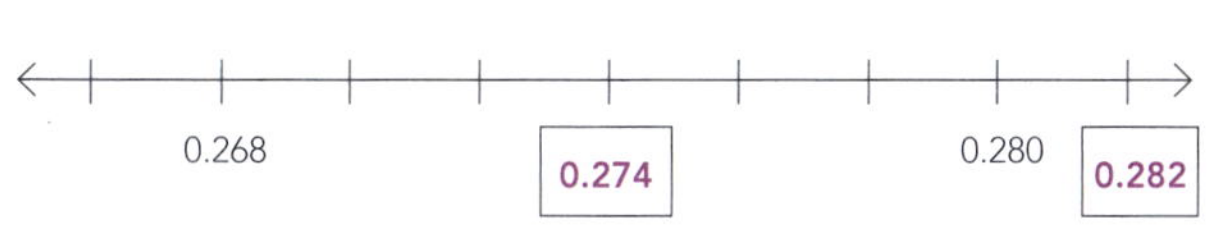

17 a $\frac{1}{3} = \frac{3}{9}$ b $25\% > \frac{1}{5}$
18 $0.\dot{4}8\dot{1}$
19 a 29 b 10001
20

	Fraction	Fraction over 100	Decimal	Percentage
a	$\frac{1}{20}$	$\frac{5}{100}$	0.05	5%
b	$\frac{3}{8}$	$\frac{37.5}{100}$	0.375	37.5%
c	$\frac{1}{40}$	$\frac{2.5}{100}$	0.025	2.5%

21 a 115 b 0.684
22 a $x = 0.\dot{7}$
$10x = 7.\dot{7}$
$9x = 7$
$x = \frac{7}{9}$
b Irrational numbers
23 0.0214%
24 7.1%
25 2.60×10^6
26 1716
27 30 chairs